Peter F

Twenty-First Century Receptions of Tolkien

Proceedings of The Tolkien Society
Winter Seminar 2021

Edited by Will Sherwood

Contents

About the Peter Roe Memorial Fund   iv

The Peter Roe Series   vi

Abbreviations   viii

Introduction
Will Sherwood   1

Middle-earth: Shadow of War as the new shadow
Jelena Filipovic   5

Artists from Middle-earth: a 21st-century dive into
J.R.R. Tolkien's Secondary World
Marie Bretagnolle   25

Nazgûl Taller Than Night: Tolkien and Speculative Realism
Nick Groom   38

Tolkien's Grave as a Site of Memory
Mina D. Lukić and Dejan M. Vukelić   58

About the Contributors   90

About the Peter Roe Memorial Fund

The Tolkien Society's seminar proceedings and other booklets are typically published under the auspices of the Peter Roe Memorial Fund, a fund in the Society's accounts that commemorates a young member who died in a traffic accident. Peter Roe, a young and very talented person joined the Society in 1979, shortly after his sixteenth birthday. He had discovered Middle-earth some time earlier, and was so inspired by it that he even developed his own system of runes, similar to the Dwarvish Angerthas, but which utilised logical sound values, matching the logical shapes of the runes. Peter was also an accomplished cartographer, and his bedroom was covered with multi-coloured maps of the journeys of the fellowship, plans of Middle-earth, and other drawings.

Peter was also a creative writer in both poetry and prose—the subject being incorporated into his own *Dwarvish Chronicles*. He was so enthusiastic about having joined the Society that he had written a letter ordering all the available back issues, and was on his way to buy envelopes when he was hit by a speeding lorry outside his home.

Sometime later, Jonathan and Lester Simons (at that time Chairman and Membership Secretary respectively) visited Peter's parents to see his room and to look at the work on which he had spent so much care and attention in such a tragically short life. It was obvious that Peter had produced, and would have continued to produce, material of such a high standard as to make a complete booklet, with poetry, calligraphy, stories and cartography. The then committee set up a special account in honour of Peter, with the consent of his parents, which would be the source of finance for the Society's special publications. Over the years a number of members have made generous donations to the fund.

The first publication to be financed by the Peter Roe Memorial Fund was *Some Light on Middle-earth* by Edward Crawford, published in 1985. Subsequent publications have been composed from papers delivered at Tolkien Society workshops and seminars, talks from guest speakers at the Annual Dinner, and collections of the best articles from past issues of *Amon Hen*, the Society's bulletin.

Dwarvish Fragments, an unfinished tale by Peter, was printed in *Mallorn* 15 (September 1980). A standalone collection of Peter's creative endeavours is currently being prepared for publication.

The Peter Roe Series

I   Edward Crawford, *Some Light on Middle-earth*, Peter Roe Series, I (Pinner: The Tolkien Society, 1985)

II   *Leaves from the Tree: Tolkien's Short Fiction*, ed. by Trevor Reynolds, Peter Roe Series, II (London: The Tolkien Society, 1991)

III   *The First and Second Ages*, ed. by Trevor Reynolds, Peter Roe Series, III (London: The Tolkien Society, 1992; Edinburgh: Luna Press Publishing 2020)

IV   *Travel and Communication in Tolkien's Worlds*, ed. by Richard Crawshaw, Peter Roe Series, IV (Swindon: The Tolkien Society, 1996)

V   *Digging Potatoes, Growing Trees: Volume One*, ed. by Helen Armstrong, Peter Roe Series, V (Swindon: The Tolkien Society, 1997)

VI   *Digging Potatoes, Growing Trees: Volume Two*, ed. by Helen Armstrong, Peter Roe Series, VI (Telford: The Tolkien Society, 1998)

VII   *Tolkien, the Sea and Scandinavia*, ed. by Richard Crawshaw, Peter Roe Series, VII (Telford: The Tolkien Society, 1999)

VIII   *The Ways of Creative Mythologies*, ed. by Maria Kuteeva, 2 vols, Peter Roe Series, VIII (Telford: The Tolkien Society, 2000)

IX   *Tolkien: A Mythology for England?*, ed. by Richard Crawshaw, Peter Roe Series, IX (Telford: The Tolkien Society, 2000)

X	*The Best of Amon Hen: Part One*, ed. by Andrew Wells, Peter Roe Series, X (Telford: The Tolkien Society, 2000)
XI	*Digging Potatoes, Growing Trees: Volume Three*, ed. by Helen Armstrong, Peter Roe Series, XI (Telford: The Tolkien Society, 2001)
XII	Kenneth Chaij, *Sindarin Lexicon*, Peter Roe Series, XII (Telford: The Tolkien Society, 2001)
XIII	*The Best of Amon Hen: Part Two*, ed. by Andrew Wells, Peter Roe Series, XIII (Telford: The Tolkien Society, 2002)
XIV	*Tolkien: Influenced and Influencing*, ed. by Matthew Vernon, Peter Roe Series, XIV (Telford: The Tolkien Society, 2005)
XV	*Freedom, Fate and Choice in Middle-earth*, ed. by Christopher Kreuzer, Peter Roe Series, XV (London: The Tolkien Society, 2012)
XVI	*Journeys & Destinations*, ed. by Ian Collier, Peter Roe Series, XVI (Wolverhampton: The Tolkien Society, 2015)
XVII	*Death and Immortality in Middle-earth*, ed. by Daniel Helen, Peter Roe Series, XVII (Edinburgh: Luna Press Publishing, 2017)
XVIII	*Poetry and Song in the works of J.R.R. Tolkien*, ed. by Anna Milon, Peter Roe Series, XVIII (Edinburgh: Luna Press Publishing, 2018)
XIX	*Tolkien the Pagan? Reading Middle-earth through a spiritual lens*, ed. by Anna Milon, Peter Roe Series, XIX (Edinburgh: Luna Press Publishing, 2019).
XX	*Adapting Tolkien*, ed. by Will Sherwood, Peter Roe Series, XX (Ediburgh, Luna Press Publishing, 2021)

Abbreviations

A&I	*The Lay of Aotrou and Itroun*, ed. by Verlyn Flieger (London: HarperCollins, 2016)
Arthur	*The Fall of Arthur,* ed. by Christopher Tolkien (London: HarperCollins, 2013; Boston: Houghton Mifflin Harcourt, 2013)
AW	*Ancrene Wisse* (Oxford: Oxford University Press, 1962)
B&L	*Beren and Lúthien*, ed. by Christopher Tolkien (London: HarperCollins, 2017)
Beowulf	*Beowulf: A Translation and Commentary, together with Sellic Spell*, ed. by Christopher Tolkien (London: HarperCollins, 2014; Boston: Houghton Mifflin Harcourt, 2014)
Bombadil	*The Adventures of Tom Bombadil and other verses from the Red Book* (London: George Allen & Unwin, 1962; Boston: Houghton Mifflin, 1962)
CoH	*The Children of Húrin*, ed. by Christopher Tolkien (London: HarperCollins, 2007; Boston: Houghton Mifflin Harcourt, 2007)
Exodus	*The Old English Exodus*, ed. by Joan Turville-Petre (Oxford: Oxford University Press, 1982)
Father Christmas	*Letters from Father Christmas*, ed. by Baillie Tolkien (London: George Allen & Unwin, 1976; Boston: Houghton Mifflin, 1976)

FoG	*The Fall of Gondolin*, ed. by Christopher Tolkien (London: HarperCollins, 2018).
FR	*The Fellowship of the Ring*
Hobbit	*The Hobbit*
Jewels	*The War of the Jewels,* ed. by Christopher Tolkien (London: HarperCollins, 1994; Boston: Houghton Mifflin, 1994)
Kullervo	*The Story of Kullervo,* ed. by Verlyn Flieger (London: HarperCollins, 2015; Boston: Houghton Mifflin Harcourt, 2016)
Lays	*The Lays of Beleriand,* ed. by Christopher Tolkien (London: George Allen & Unwin, 1985; Boston: Houghton Mifflin, 1985)
Letters	*The Letters of J.R.R. Tolkien,* ed. by Humphrey Carpenter with the assistance of Christopher Tolkien (London: George Allen & Unwin, 1981; Boston: Houghton Mifflin, 1981)
Lost Road	*The Lost Road and Other Writings*, ed. by Christopher Tolkien (London: Unwin Hyman, 1987; Boston: Houghton Mifflin, 1987)
Lost Tales I	*The Book of Lost Tales, Part One,* ed. by Christopher Tolkien (London: George Allen & Unwin, 1983; Boston: Houghton Mifflin, 1984)
Lost Tales II	*The Book of Lost Tales, Part Two*, ed. by Christopher Tolkien (London: George Allen & Unwin, 1984; Boston: Houghton Mifflin, 1984)

Monsters	*The Monsters and the Critics and Other Essays* (London: George Allen & Unwin, 1983; Boston: Houghton Mifflin, 1984)
Morgoth	*Morgoth's Ring*, ed. by Christopher Tolkien (London: Geore, 1993; Boston: Houghton Mifflin, 1993)
OFS	*Tolkien On Fairy-stories*, ed. by Verlyn Flieger and Douglas A. Anderson (London: HarperCollins, 2008)
P&S	*Poems and Stories* (London: George Allen & Unwin, 1980; Boston: Houghton Mifflin, 1994)
Peoples	*The Peoples of Middle-earth*, ed. by Christopher Tolkien (London: HarperCollins, 1996; Boston: Houghton Mifflin, 1996)
Perilous Realm	*Tales from the Perilous Realm* (London: HarperCollins, 1997)
RK	*The Return of the King*
Silmarillion	*The Silmarillion*, ed. by Christopher Tolkien (London: George Allen & Unwin, 1977; Boston: Houghton Mifflin, 1977).
Sauron	*Sauron Defeated*, ed. by Christopher Tolkien (London: HarperCollins, 1992; Boston: Houghton Mifflin, 1992)
Secret Vice	*A Secret Vice: Tolkien on Invented Languages*, ed. by Dimitra Fimi and Andrew Higgins (London: HarperCollins, 2016)

Shadow	*The Return of the Shadow*, ed. by Christopher Tolkien (London: Unwin Hyman, 1988; Boston: Houghton Mifflin, 1988)
Shaping	*The Shaping of Middle-earth*, ed. by Christopher Tolkien (London: George Allen & Unwin, 1986; Boston: Houghton Mifflin, 1986)
S&G	*The Legend of Sigurd and Gudrún*, ed. by Christopher Tolkien (London: HarperCollins, 2009; Boston: Houghton Mifflin Harcourt, 2009)
TL	*Tree and Leaf*, 2nd edn (London: Unwin Hyman, 1988; Boston: Houghton Mifflin, 1989)
TT	*The Two Towers*
Treason	*The Treason of Isengard*, ed. by Christopher Tolkien (London: Unwin Hyman; Boston: Houghton Mifflin, 1989)
UT	*Unfinished Tales of Númenor and Middle-earth*, ed. by Christopher Tolkien (London: George Allen & Unwin, 1980; Boston: Houghton Mifflin, 1980)
War	*The War of the Ring*, ed. by Christopher Tolkien (London: Unwin Hyman, 1990; Boston: Houghton Mifflin, 1990)

Introduction

Will Sherwood

"I find that many children become interested, even engrossed, in *The Lord of the Rings*, from about 10 onwards. I think it rather a pity, really. It was not written for them. But then I am a very 'unvoracious' reader, and since I can seldom bring myself to read a work twice I think of the many things that I read – too soon!" (*Letters*, Letter 189, 249)

J.R.R. Tolkien's name erupted into the twenty-first century with Peter Jackson's adaption of *The Lord of the Rings* (2001–3), bringing new waves of readers to the Professor's world of Middle-earth. The staggering range of art, film, fan fiction, video games, and music that has been produced and admired by the Tolkien community since the turn of the millennium proves Tolkien's continuing appeal. Additionally, the list of published works by Tolkien has substantially expanded, introducing the public to new material that has since been collected, consumed, and discussed. Most notably, this is not always by academics. Twenty-first century studies on reception theory evidences fan culture's value and aim to broaden the horizon and attention of Tolkien scholarship.

As a case and study, it is not unfamiliar to Tolkien's readers that *The Hobbit*'s sequel slowly transformed from a children's story into a darker, adult-oriented narrative. As shown in the epigraph above, the author appeared to react to young people reading *The Lord of the Rings* negatively; it was not *supposed* to be received by young people. Verlyn Flieger counters Tolkien's perspective here by explaining that although *LotR* "is not primarily directed at children, nor is it designed primarily to interest them . . . it is certainly literature for children" (148). Most recently, this has been supported and explored by Luke Shelton in his PhD: '*Small Hands Do Them Because They Must': examining the reception of The Lord of the Rings among young readers* (2020) which justifies why the views and discussions of young readers are just as valid as our own.

Tolkien famously declared that he wanted "other minds and hands, wielding paint and music and drama" to develop and embellish on his "scheme" (*Letters*, Letter 131, 145) and although some modes of adaption were examined during the seminar, the twenty-first century has birthed new modes of thinking such as Speculative Realism that germinated from the conference held at Goldsmiths College, University of London in 2007. Graham Harman's Object-Oriented Ontology grants readers an opportunity to move beyond the Anthropocene to consider how there is an "additional reality" and "'potentiality'" to our world (and by extension Middle-earth) that is yet to be examined (103). It may be possible that contemporary modes of thinking may help us to read Tolkien in new ways, ways that may help us with our own concerns (such as global warming).

The Tolkien Society 2021 winter seminar, which took place on the 13th of February, continued the Society's devotion to providing the public with free access to research into Tolkien's life and works by being held solely online. The online platform proved yet again (following the 2020 *Adapting Tolkien* seminar) that online/hybrid events allow for greater engagement from the Tolkien community. Over five-hundred attendees and speakers from across the globe were welcomed on Zoom and YouTube.

In order to accommodate as many time zones as possible, the event was condensed in size with only twelve papers.

Of the twelve papers, four are presented in this proceedings. Jelena Filipovic opens with an exploration of the *Middle-earth: Shadow of War* video game, tying its depiction of morality and evil to Tolkien's unfinished sequel 'The New Shadow'. Marie Bretagnolle follows by examining the works of four twenty-first century artists: Alan Lee, John Howe, Tómas Hijo, and Jay Johnstone. Nick Groom introduces us to Speculative Realism, examining the "additional reality" of Middle-earth and how Tolkien's writing communicates with the broader ideas of the twenty-first century Anthropocene. Mina D. Lukić, and Dejan M. Vukelić conclude with an assessment of how Tolkien's grave in Oxford operates as a site of memory, offering visitors an endless range of opportunities to engage with and interpret the site as they wish.

On behalf of the Tolkien Society, I would like to extend my deepest gratitude to the presenters of the Tolkien Society 2021 winter seminar, without whom the event would not have happened. I would also like to thank the Society's committee for their continued support and guidance in the planning and running of the event, and the publishing of this proceedings. The publication itself is made possible by the generosity of the Peter Roe Memorial Fund, for which I am grateful.

Bibliography

Flieger, Verlyn, *Splintered Light: Logos and Language in Tolkien's World*, (Kent: Kent State University Press, 2002).

Harman, Graham, *Towards Speculative Realism: Essays and Lectures*. (Winchester: Zero Books, 2010).

Tolkien, J.R.R., *The Letters of J.R.R. Tolkien*, ed. Humphrey Carpenter with the assistance of Christopher Tolkien (London: HarperCollins, 2006).

Middle-earth: Shadow of War
as the new shadow

Jelena Filipovic

The video game *Middle-earth: Shadow of War* (2017) takes place in an alternate storyworld that depicts events preceding *LotR* and yet it does testimony to the very danger Tolkien had envisioned for a possible sequel to *LotR* when he said, "it is inevitable that we should be concerned with the most regrettable feature of [man's] nature: their quick satiety with good" (*Letters*, Letter 256, 344).[1] *SoW* sheds a new light on Tolkien's conception of morality throughout the legendarium, but threatens it at the same time. The problematic that gradually articulated itself in Tolkien's 'The New Shadow' (and which the author had predicted) occurs on a structural and thematic level. One way of looking at Tolkien's assertion that the narrative would not be worth doing is that the structure of the new narrative would follow *LotR* too closely; there would be an evil once again which would need to be defeated and although it might be situated in a different place, at a different time, with different protagonists, the story would have a similar outcome. On the thematic level, 'The New Shadow' would not be worth pursuing because after Sauron's defeat in *LotR* there is no longer a divine, angelic enemy in Middle-earth and all future conflicts in Middle-earth would be tedious.

---

1. *Middle-earth: Shadow of War* is hereafter abbreviated to *SoW*.

SoW tells the story of Talion, a non-canonical Ranger, who is brought back from the dead by the wraith of Celebrimbor. By using Talion as his vessel, Celebrimbor aims to get revenge on Sauron for having deceived the Elves in matters concerning the making of the Rings of Power and ultimately free Middle-earth from the Dark Lord. In the first game, *Middle-earth: Shadow of Mordor* (2014), Talion/Celebrimbor uses his powers to start a civil war among the Orcs in an attempt to take the throne from Sauron.[2] In *SoW*, it becomes clear that Celebrimbor's priority is to amass power to use against Sauron rather than save lives, as Talion struggles to do. Talion and Celebrimbor begin the second game on Mount Doom, where they have forged a new ring to challenge the One Ring. Both games apply a deconstructive approach to Tolkien's storytelling. They explore the idea of fighting Sauron from within Mordor, using his means, his creatures, and his weapons. This involves enslaving the Orcs by magic, and encouraging their worst impulses of warfare, competition, and cut-throat violence which Talion/Celebrimbor subverts to his own end.

The game expresses a diabolical dualism of Dark Lord (Sauron) vs Bright Lord (Celebrimbor) and its gameplay focuses heavily on the anti-villain trope – the protagonist embodies virtuous, heroic traits and goals, but his means at attaining them are morally ambiguous. At the core of this problematic where good and evil seem to merge is René Girard's anthropological concept of mimetic rivalry. This is a paradox that occurs when antagonists confront one another so implacably that they begin to resemble one another more and more. The initial differences that separated them are now dissolved.

---

2. *Middle-earth: Shadow of Mordor* is hereafter abbreviated to *SoM*.

Mimetic rivalry is the principal source of violence between human beings, which results from imitation of a model who becomes a rival or, vice versa, of a rival who becomes a model. Rivalries can be political, economic, athletic, sexual, artistic, intellectual, religious. Girard uses the word "scandal" to summarize mimetic rivalry and its consequences, one party is always scandalized by the other because it sees this other as an obstacle (Girard 2001, 16). However, it is a paradoxical obstacle because it repels and attracts at the same time: mimetic rivalries who mutually prevent each other from appropriating the object of desire reinforce more and more their double desire – their desire for the other's object of desire and for the desire of the other. The object is not always necessarily the same either. Celebrimbor desires peace for Middle-earth, while Sauron desires dominion. Although, the game shows that there is a very thin line (or none at all) between peace and dominion.

When one scandal occurs, it gives rise to another, resulting in various crises which proliferate unceasingly and become all the more violent. This is why Girard speaks of mimetic "contagion" (19). In the first stage the contagion divides, fragments and decomposes communities and then later it gathers all those scandalized to act against one single victim (= the scapegoat). This is a process that begins with desire and rivalry. As the rivalries/scandals multiply, they create a violent crisis – the war of all against all. This war of all against all would annihilate the entire community unless its violence is transformed into a war against one, which re-establishes the initial unity. Violence must intensify and escalate in order to produce its own antidote.

'The New Shadow'

I have briefly mentioned above how 'The New Shadow' as a narrative in its own right, has the potential of repeating that which its prequel, *LotR*, had already exhaustively illustrated. The story would once again incorporate the main building blocks of "plot", "discovery" and "overthrow" (*Letters*, Letter 256, 344). Furthermore, with both the presence and potency of the main divine antagonist (Sauron) removed from the stage, all proceeding antagonistic agencies, such as political enemies, would not be interesting and all in all not worth recounting as Tolkien explains in Letter 338. This is the "deeper conviction" Christopher Tolkien refers to when he states that "the vast structure of story, in many forms, that he [Tolkien] had raised came to its true end in the Downfall of Sauron" (*Peoples*, 418). Yet beyond the structural and thematic argumentation there seems to lie another reasoning as to why Tolkien abandoned this sequel, one which he does not express directly but can nevertheless be read in-between the lines of his letters. Ironically, this would have given the story its very fuel, had it been further developed.

When Tolkien says his sequel "proved both sinister and depressing", this may not only be limited to the genre or theme of the story (*Letters*, Letter 256, 344). It can also be understood in terms of morality. He mentions "Satanistic religion" and "dark cults" which are (and this is truly the sinister bit) not strictly allocated to the side of Tolkien's usual agents of evil but to the good side – the good people of Gondor (344). Peace, justice, and prosperity eventually become boring and Men will be satiated with the good. This is the restlessness which Tolkien says is inevitable and which he consciously decided not to put on paper, for better or for worse. Despite having abandoned the narrative, Tolkien had composed a few introductory pages to 'The New Shadow' which already set the sinister atmosphere.

The story opens with an old man, Borlas, contemplating the nature of Evil in an almost monological manner until the next main character is introduced shortly after, a young man called Saelon, who questions and counters Borlas' beliefs. The text develops into a dialogue between Borlas and Saelon, reminiscent of such philosophical conversations between two characters in Tolkien's legendarium as in the case of 'The Debate of Finrod and Andreth'. It has even more striking similarities to the father-son dialogue between Elendil and Herendil in *The Lost Road* (1987). In both dialogues, from *Lost Road* and 'The New Shadow', Tolkien stages generational discrepancies when profound topics are discussed: what is right, what is wrong, the past, and the current socio-political state of affairs. Also, both dialogues contain a foreshadowing of some greater evil yet to come.

The major difference is that the conversation between Borlas and Saelon does not finish on a note of reconciliation as does that between Elendil and Herendil. This is mainly due to the fact that Saelon is a sinister character who seems to have ulterior motives. The idea of a 'new shadow', Tolkien's theme of the inevitable perpetuation of evil, gradually emerges through and is contained in Saelon's arguments. He has had a deep resentment towards Borlas since childhood; he accuses people of being hypocrites; in the end he refers to a notorious figure known as "Herumor" and hints at conspiratorial behaviour among citizens (*Peoples*, 414).

What is more, the name Saelon has an uncanny resemblance

to Sauron, which I do not think is merely coincidental.[3] This is not to say that this character is some new form of Sauron himself, but rather that "the roots of Evil" (411), one could say the seeds and fruit of Melkor (to keep with the imagery of trees and whose name Borlas uses throughout the text), are deeply embedded in the storyworld and will always resurface, one way or another.[4] Yet Tolkien does leave space for mystery concerning Saelon's character and his connection to the supernatural is not necessarily ruled out as he says "I have eyes and ears, *and other senses*, Master." (414; emphasis added). It is also worth mentioning that this sentence is the only instance where Saelon does not refer to his addressee as Master Borlas, but just Master, which gives it a dubious undertone that is unlike one good character to refer to another as "Master" (414).

Saelon voices opinions similar to those of younger Númenórean generations in *Lost Road* about being bored with the ongoing idyllic state of their society.[5] In Gondor's current state there is growing discontent, as Saelon points out, "Not all are content since the Great King died, and fewer now are afraid" (414). Borlas' son, Berelach, reveals more of this negativity in the letter to his father: "Peace makes things slack" (417). The story so far does not provide concrete information about the

---

3. Another resemblance is to Satan, which is not arbitrary given Saelon's inquisitive role as one who tempts and tests Borlas.

4. Tolkien could have just as well applied Melkor/Morgoth instead of the word Evil, but since the Dark Lord is off the narrative stage, Tolkien places a word that may still refer to him. All evil is in some way connected to Melkor; Melkor is Evil, Evil is Melkor.

5. In *Lost Road* Christopher Tolkien notes "Númenor is seen by the young people as over-populous, boring, 'over-known': 'every tree and grass-blade is counted', in Herendil's words; and this cause of discontent is used, it seems, by Sauron" (77).

situation in or around Gondor, it is only revealed through subtle remarks, which does justice to the word 'shadow' in the title. In these early stages of the story the 'shadow' gradually crystalizes, mainly through Saelon's arguments, but also through Borlas' worry and the depiction of a change in weather.[6] Saelon and Berelach are both members of a younger generation which seems to be heedless of past events and Borlas, being an old man who remembers the War of the Ring, is set in contrast to them. Tolkien illustrates how the new shadow arises within the *new* generation and those who "remembered the Evil of old" are seen as a threat that needs to be eliminated (417).

Although 'The New Shadow' only consists of a few pages, it already opens a window into the problematic concerning the fallible nature of humanity. No matter how blissful and righteous a state they find themselves in, there is always that Melkor-ingredient, even in the best of them, that resurfaces sooner or later. The serpentine arguments Saelon produces and the discourse that arises are the very Shadow itself in rhetorical form, even in the heart of Borlas' own Eden-like garden where the conversation takes place. The shadow may be new in regard to time and space, but it is a shadow or rather *the* Shadow nonetheless.

2. An un-Tolkienesque dualism

Although Talion is the protagonist of *SoW* through whom the player navigates the game world, it is the antagonistic dualism

---

6. Tolkien creates this suspenseful, foreboding atmosphere in the conversation between Elendil and Herendil just prior to Númenor's catastrophic downfall. A similar atmosphere is also present in the chapter 'The *Shadow* of the Past' of *LotR*.

between Celebrimbor and Sauron which highlights Girard's mimetic contagion. Following canon, which borrows from 'Of the Rings of Power' and fragments from 'The History of Galadriel and Celeborn', the two characters begin as enemies in *SoM* and they stay enemies until the end of *SoW*. In the latter it becomes apparent that the more violent (and this not only in the physical sense) the enmity between Celebrimbor and Sauron, the more they lack difference, and the more Celebrimbor turns into an antagonist himself.

The beginning of the game depicts Celebrimbor forging a new ring, apparently equal in power to the One Ring. This is the first act in *SoW* that signifies mimetic contagion in that Celebrimbor imitates his enemy through this very act of creation, regardless of Celebrimbor's conviction that his aims are justified. To begin with, we can view the One Ring as Girard's idea of the scandal. On the one hand, there are those who 'accept' the Ring and those who reject it. This is related to Tolkien's statement that there is no inherent dualism in his legendarium. The good-vs-evil is always a "conscious reaction" which comes about, in this case, as a result of the scandal (Tolkien 1964). The scandal, therefore, can have a polarizing effect for the better, by distinguishing those who accept the Ring, side with it, and those who do not.

On the other hand, it can be polarizing for the worse in that it turns individuals against one another. They enter into mutual conflict and in some cases even into self-conflict (e.g. Gollum). This is where the contagion-mechanism is triggered. The Ring attracts all kinds of individuals, even ones completely indifferent to each other. Its "hostility becomes so contagious that it spreads to the most diverse individuals" (Girard 2001, 19). This is the "power of mimetic attraction" of the scandal (23).

In a paradoxical way, the contagion "divides and fragments" but also "gathers and reunites" which is exactly the nature of Sauron's Ring (22). *SoW* does not focus on this mechanism concerning Celebrimbor's new ring. Yet the contagion lies in Celebrimbor's very act of having created another scandal (the new ring is a scandal from Sauron's point of view) to counter the original scandal (the One Ring). Celebrimbor's act is still within the logic of contagious mimetic behaviour and therefore cannot pose as a solution to the contagion. The idea of a new Ring being diabolical may be implied in the game, but it is never explicitly condemned as such. The problem with the adjective 'new' is that it is just not that. The new Ring is about as new as the *new* Shadow. It is, in fact, the same *old* diabolical power that is at work. In 'The New Shadow', Borlas is able to recognize this: "he smelt the old Evil and knew it for what it was" (*Peoples*, 418).

The parallels between Celebrimbor and Sauron do not begin with Celebrimbor's imitation of Sauron. The game implements the canonical history of the characters from Tolkien's legendarium. Celebrimbor was a master in smithery and craftsmanship from the beginning and had created other Rings of Power prior to the creation of the new Ring in *SoW*. None of these attributes and acts, however, were a means that Celebrimbor had utilized to achieve a certain end. His skill in craft is in itself a beneficial and untainted talent, something Tolkien imparts on most of his characters, and the three Elven Rings of Power are primarily manifestations of that positive trait – art for art's sake – that do not serve a purpose as does the One Ring. This crucial difference between Celebrimbor and Sauron is diminished in *SoW* when the former begins to do exactly what the latter had done: use his skill to create a powerful object which will serve as a means to reclaim the government of Middle-earth.

Once the new ring is forged it becomes an essential feature not only for the plot of *SoW*, but for the gameplay itself. The player is able to use the ring to 'Dominate' enemies. This is an idiosyncratic feature of both *SoM* and *SoW* where Talion/Celebrimbor can subvert Orcs, Trolls, Caragors, and even Drakes, to fight on his side by controlling their minds, i.e. dominating their wills, which is a literal portrayal of the domination-power ascribed to the Ring in the *LotR* books. By emitting a bright, silvery-blueish light, the inscription carved into the new ring, as well as its influence over dominated creatures, is opposed to the golden One Ring that emits a fiery red colour. The aesthetic of the new ring is reflected in Celebrimbor's new title as Bright Lord, another binary opposition to Sauron's title of Dark Lord.

However, the latter's title is not his own. It is imparted onto him by his enemies who refer to him in that way, as do his servants occasionally. Celebrimbor bestows the title Bright Lord onto himself by himself. With this new title he gains a new identity, but not in the positive sense Tolkien ascribes to his characters under the term "'ennoblement'", in Celebrimbor's case it is rather a degradation that cements him in mimetic rivalry (*Letters*, Letter 180, 232). He becomes a new Sauron, which in turn does nothing to counteract the original Sauron, rather it amplifies Sauron's diabolical presence through this act of mimesis.[7]

Yet ironically, the more confident Celebrimbor becomes

---

7. I use the word 'diabolical' in the strict sense of referring to two-ness, two-sidedness, split. The Greek term for 'devil' is *dia-bolos*.

in the game of warfare, to the point where he feels complete autonomy has been gained and his actions are no longer dependant on his rival Sauron, who is also his model, the more this autonomy is "a reflection of the illusions projected by [his] admiration for them" (Girard 2001, 15). Celebrimbor subsequently becomes all the more enslaved to Sauron. Celebrimbor's acceptance of Sauron's illusiveness is also not non-canonical, however. In *Unfinished Tales of Númenor and Middle-earth* (1980), it is mentioned that although "Celebrimbor was not corrupted in heart or faith", he "accepted Sauron as what he posed to be" (*UT*, 306). Yet the innocence of Celebrimbor coupled with Sauron's deceitful "machinations" are not the only reason for the Noldorin smith's acceptance of Sauron (305). There is also Celebrimbor's own "obsession with crafts" (394), an untainted talent one could say, which is the defining factor as to why he accepts Sauron. In fact, Sauron hardly needs to exercise any form of manipulation at all, he rather functions as a mirror in which Celebrimbor sees himself. It is a very Tolkienian characteristic that the Dark Lord does not actually use one's weaknesses against one (these are already his) but rather one's strengths.

3. Talion the scapegoat

So far, the main focus of my analysis has been the mimetic rivalry between Celebrimbor and Sauron, but what role does the game's main protagonist Talion fulfil in the struggle to restore order? The answer to this question will also be the answer to the crucial question regarding the end of the mimetic violence, or violence in general, between the Bright Lord and the Dark Lord. In his theory Girard introduces the concept of the single victim mechanism. This mechanism operates within the ritual act of sacrifice. Girard sees sacrifice and scapegoating as two different expressions of the same reality. Both sacrifice and scapegoat are victims, whether human or animal. The ultimate goal of sacrificing or expelling a victim is to regain "relief from the stress of conflict and violence" within a community or party (Girard 2001, xv). That is why in the Bible the ritual of scapegoating involves transferring the sins of a people onto a male goat and driving him into the wilderness.

Talion, the male human being, is caught in the violence between Elf (Celebrimbor) and Maia (Sauron). His story in *SoM* begins with loss. His garrison stationed at the Black Gate of Mordor is overthrown and he is tragically forced to watch the death of his family. These introductory events in the game already set the single victim mechanism that is to be carried out with Talion acting as that victim. The Black Hand of Sauron performs a real ritualistic sacrifice by killing Talion's family and Talion himself in order to summon the spirit (wraith) of Celebrimbor into the Black Hand's own body. The sacrifice backfires and Celebrimbor merges with Talion instead.

Now although this is a very real and literal sacrifice, the sacrifice Girard speaks of is a collective act (the majority is always against the victim) of eliminating the victim/scapegoat in order to restore some kind of original order which a scandal had disturbed. In *SoM*, Talion's sacrifice is not fully in accordance with Girard's theory yet. There does not seem to be a collective violence coming from a diverse majority who want Talion dead, unless the three Black Captains present at the ritual count as a majority. The ritual also does not aim at restoring any particular order, yet it does summon the spirit of Celebrimbor back into a body, which is the only act of restoration here.

In *SoW*, there is a continuation of the collective violence against Talion. Talion realizes that Celebrimbor, as the latter also admits, has used Talion's body this entire time for personal gain rather than to cooperate with him and save Middle-earth together. Celebrimbor's aim is to save Middle-earth *from Sauron* and replace him as the Bright Lord. When Talion refuses to comply with Celebrimbor, his role as Celebrimbor's ring-bearer and bodily vessel is taken over by Eltariel.[8] Having no Ring of Power to sustain his life, Talion is left to die. Once again there is a collective violence of a majority, represented here in the Elvish alliance between Celebrimbor and Eltariel, that is set against the single victim, the man Talion. He is once again sacrificed for a greater cause and yet unlike the first time this sacrifice is not ritualistic, it is anti-climactic betrayal. In *SoM*, Talion's sacrifice is instigated by Sauron in an attempt to summon Celebrimbor, gain mastery over him, and govern Middle-earth; in *SoW*, Talion poses as an obstacle to Celebrimbor who sacrifices him in order to dominate Sauron and restore order to Middle-earth. Talion serves as the scapegoat in both cases for the same reasons.

However, Talion's sacrifice is not finalized until the very end of the game. Once Celebrimbor and Eltariel leave him to die, he takes Isildur's ring and in doing so is able to stay alive. Eventually, he gives in to this ring's power and becomes himself one of the Nine, replacing Isildur.[9] It is in this ultimate conversion, from being the main protagonist in the game series to one of the major antagonists in *LotR* – a kind of fall,

8. Eltariel is a minor character in the game, an Elf-assassin sent by Galadriel to help in the fight for Middle-earth.

9. In the game, Isildur is retrospectively portrayed as having fallen victim to Sauron and having accepted one of the Nine Rings, thus becoming a Nazgûl.

that Talion is victimized. He is sacrificed by both sides as the scapegoat whose elimination is meant to restore a given order. Although he chooses a third way, by submitting neither to Sauron's nor Celebrimbor's violence, *SoW* does not portray Talion's decision as a solution to the contagion of mimetic violence. Why did the writers and producers of the game decide that Talion should turn into a Nazgûl in the end? Is it a realistic consequence of his having been under the influence of a Ring of Power that is supposed to rebuke the illusion of unrealistic, romantic, wishful longing for a typical happy ending? Does the event provide a heartfelt background story to one of Tolkien's Nazgûl that allows us not to view him *a priori* evil?

I believe that the answer to the last two questions is affirmative, and there is nothing wrong with that as such. The problem is, as mentioned above, that *SoW* does not allow Talion to break through the violence. By taking one of the Nine Rings to sustain his life so that he could continue defending Minas Ithil and the people of Gondor (indeed a selfless and virtuous act), one begs the question whether he is really sacrificing himself or rather being seduced by the possibility which a Sauronic ring offers. To have really made a sacrifice, Talion would not have taken up the ring and instead died an honourable death, not one as a Ringwraith (but that would be another story and another game altogether). The last scene in *SoW* does depict Talion as redeemed, yet this redemption lacks the inevitable sacrifice that Tolkien makes his characters undergo in order to reach that cathartic state. In *LotR* there is also no hero who destroys the Ring and saves Middle-earth, the Ring's undoing comes about through sacrifice. Without this factor, the 'third way' is nothing but Sauron's way once again. It is just a new way, much like the new Shadow.

4. Perpetual War

A final aspect worth considering is the very war itself in the game. The game hinges on the idea that it is necessary to keep Mordor in a constant state of war at all costs. This does not mean one particular war that consists of two sides, but a war of all against all. This infamous postulation of perpetual war harks back to Thomas Hobbes' political theory in his seminal work *Leviathan* (1651). Hobbes rebukes the idea that humans are naturally social creatures and states that "without a common power to keep them in awe, Men are in a state of War" that "is not only fighting, but the accumulation of all things that lead up to that" (Hobbes 1985, 185-6). The Hobbesian state of nature is a state of war. It is a time of crisis, permanent fear and mistrust of individuals against one another, in which rules have broken down and there is no governing authority to keep people in check. There is, coming from all sides, a will to engage in conflict.

In *SoW*, the Hobbesian state of war plays out most vividly in the case of the Orcs. Both *SoM* and *SoW* are unique for their implementation of the Nemesis system. The Nemesis system is "essentially a rotation of rivals that players fight and defeat throughout the game" (Dolen 2020). A Nemesis can be any Uruk or Olog-Hai who has gained recognition within the Orc hierarchy. There is a military and social hierarchy among Orcs in *SoW* where they can rise in rank or be demoted, and they are organized in various tribes.[10] Talion is tasked with killing or recruiting various Orc Captains, Warchiefs, Overlords

---

10. Dark Tribe, Feral Tribe, Machine Tribe, Marauder Tribe, Mystic Tribe, Terror Tribe, Warmonger Tribe, Slaughter Tribe.

to oppose Sauron's Orc armies. With the rise of Talion/ Celebrimbor's Orc army in numbers, they are constantly in conflict with Sauron's. Even among the Orcs themselves who may be of the same party, there is envy, treachery, distrust and it is not unlikely for an Orc to kill another in order to excel in ranking. The same antagonism functions on the individual level between Celebrimbor and Sauron who unceasingly vie for power as Lord of Middle-earth. Talion's aim is to keep all of Mordor in a Hobbesian state of perpetual war so that no one party has the upper hand.[11]

SoM and *SoW* emphasize the role of Orcs both on the geopolitical scale of war and on the more individual level where Orcs like Ratbag and Bruz become decisive agents throughout the gameplay. The insight into Orcs' lives, their personalities, dynamic relationships among themselves and with Talion/the player, certainly makes the games all the more interesting. This kind of representation is also a counter-response to the stereotypical criticism that Tolkien portrays Orcs as base, brutish, passive agents and as the demonized Other. The games lend the Orcs their own stories and emotion.

Be that as it may, I see a latent danger in such a representation as it downplays the real threat that Tolkien's Evil poses and allows the player to find it interesting and, at some point, sympathise with it. This is not to say that Orcs must be automatically viewed and treated by us in an Orcish

11. Some Orcs go so far as to even challenge Sauron. Zog is a necromancer who practices the dark arts as a member of the Mystic Tribe. He and his acolytes aim to resurrect the Balrog Tar Goroth, dominate and use him to oppose Sauron. The Mystic faction of the Orcs and their practice of dark magic is clearly the game's use of Tolkien's idea of Orc cults that arise in Middle-earth after Sauron's downfall.

manner, but it also does not imply that Orcish-ness should be deconstructed in its entirety or endorsed. This is exactly the danger Tolkien envisions in 'The New Shadow' when "Gondorian boys [start] playing at being Orcs and going around doing damage" (*Letters*, Letter 256, 344). The more one is exposed to or immerses themselves in that Evil, the likelier they are to accept it. Humans begin to lose their humanity and in imitating Orcs gradually become them.[12]

Further enmity is pitted between Elves and Men. Talion and Celebrimbor begin as allies in the game and their friendship represents the bond between the two races who, despite their many differences, share a common enemy in the form of the Dark Lord. In *SoW* this bond is fractured as Celebrimbor pursues a totalitarian rulership over Middle-earth and Talion chooses a 'third way'. Nor is this factor limited to Talion and Celebrimbor. Eltariel, the other Elf character, also forsakes Talion in the end when she becomes Celebrimbor's new vessel, leaving Talion to die. Also, unlike Galadriel who functions as a redeemer for herself and her people, Eltariel's character undergoes a development in the opposite direction. *SoW* thus vilifies Elves and turns them against Men through its portrayal of Celebrimbor and Eltariel's desertion of Talion. This is not the first time there is enmity between the races in Tolkien's universe, but in Tolkien's writings this vilification is always instigated by the Shadow (e.g., Sauron in Númenor). In *SoW*, it does not come about as a result of manipulation, but rather springs from the protagonists themselves. It is the inevitable unravelling of the anti-villain strand in Celebrimbor and, ultimately, Eltariel.

---

12. This may be why Saelon detests the parallel Borlas draws between his Saleon's behaviour and that of Orcs.

One final point worth considering is a notion that is central to Hobbes' political theory: the sovereign, also known as the Leviathan. In order put an end to the condition of constant fear, distrust and insecurity, people enter into a covenant with one another and reach an agreement about the need to submit to the strongest power. The agreement is not derived from a rational desire for peace, but from fear. It takes the emergence of a sovereign-representative (one individual or a group of individuals) to truly guarantee unity and peace. In *SoW*, Sauron is this sovereign. Throughout the game, especially in Shelob's commentary, Sauron is depicted as one who first and foremost wants to bring order – which is in line with Tolkien's own analysis and close reading of Sauron.[13] Hobbes' sovereign is not only a political leader, but also a mortal god. Sauron may not be mortal, but he does exhibit divine/godlike qualities due to his angelic nature. Sauron, the sovereign, brings about order to the ongoing state of war among the inhabitants of Middle-earth by accumulating all forces under his sovereignty. Talion, on the other hand, aims to keep Mordor in a perpetual state of war (Sauron's Orc factions fighting against Celebrimbor's) since only then can the exertion of the war onto the rest of Middle-earth be avoided.

All in all, *SoW* encapsulates that flawed nature of humans and the inversion of good and evil which Tolkien had set for 'The New Shadow'. The sequel shows how versatile the Shadow is, whether that's Sauron or Melkor himself, and that to regenerate and take shape it does not need to do so physically. In *SoW*, the protagonists eventually all become bad or they die. And major antagonists, such as Shelob are portrayed as good. Although

13. See *Morgoth's Ring* (1993).

the game does not endorse but rather exposes the problems that are staged in 'The New Shadow', it does not offer, morally speaking, a better alternative to counter the Shadow. I do not see the game's solution to violence and war by keeping good/ evil in balance as palpable.

Bibliography

Dolen, Rob, *What Happened to the Nemesis System in Video Games*, 14 August 2020, https://gamerant.com/video-games-nemesis-system/ [accessed 25 March 2021].

Girard, René, *I See Satan Fall Like Lightning*, trans. James G. Williams, (Maryknoll: Orbis Books, 2001).

Hobbes, Thomas, *Leviathan*, (London: Penguin Books, 1985).

Middle-earth: Shadow of Mordor, develop. Monolith Productions (Warner Bros. Interactive Entertainment, 2014).

Middle-earth: Shadow of War, develop. Monolith Productions, (Warner Bros. Interactive Entertainment, 2017).

Tolkien, J.R.R., *The Letters of J.R.R. Tolkien*, ed. Humphrey Carpenter with the assistance of Christopher Tolkien, (London: HarperCollins, 2006).

Tolkien, J.R.R., *The Fellowship of the Ring*, (London: HarperCollins, 2008).
— *Unfinished Tales of Númenor and Middle-earth*, (London: HarperCollins, 2014).
— *The Lost Road and Other Writings*, ed. Christopher Tolkien, (London: HarperCollins, 2015).
— *Morgoth's Ring*, ed. Christopher Tolkien, (London: HarperCollins, 2015).
— *The Peoples of Middle-earth*, ed. Christopher Tolkien, (London: HarperCollins, 2015).

Artists from Middle-earth: a 21st-century dive into J.R.R. Tolkien's Secondary World [1]

Marie Bretagnolle

This paper was partly inspired by an interview of Tómas Hijo by the Tolkien Collector's Guide. In this interview, Hijo explained:

> I looked for a technique for portraying Middle-earth 'from inside'. … I didn't want to 'photograph' Middle-earth, I wanted to recreate it like a Hobbit from the Shire or a Dwarf from Erebor would do. I wanted to do 'art from Middle-earth', not 'art about Middle-earth'.[2]

Hijo's approach is inspired by J.R.R. Tolkien himself. It creates bridges between the Primary world (our own) and the Secondary world (Middle-earth). This paper explores what it means for an artist working in traditional mediums like paints, pencils, or a printing press, to present their art as coming "from" Middle-earth, offering the viewers a dive in the Secondary world unlike what an illustration usually sets out to do. Four

---

1. A translation of this paper in French is available on my blog at: https://voirtolkien.hypotheses.org/ [accessed 15 March 2021].
2. See the artist's interview by the Tolkien Collector's Guide here: https://www.tolkienguide.com/modules/newbb/viewtopic.php?topic_id=3715&forum=12&post_id=25543#forumpost25543 [accessed 15 March 2021].

artists are my focus here: Alan Lee, John Howe, Tómas Hijo, and Jay Johnstone. They all embody in their own way artistic approaches to Middle-earth that, as far as I know, were mostly explored since the beginning of the 21st century. Lee and Howe present themselves as travellers, Hijo recreates artworks that could have been produced in Middle-earth, and last but not least, Johnstone draws analogies between art history from our world, and representations of characters created by Tolkien.

Artists as travellers

When John Howe published his *Middle-earth Traveller* in 2018, he subtitled it "Sketches from Bag End to Mordor". He put emphasis on the idea of a journey made by the author and artist, pencil in hand,[3] across Middle-earth and beyond. His book is a visual guide: it presents drawings and paintings alongside short explanatory paragraphs about the history of such or such location.

His book is in the direct line of Lee's *Lord of the Rings Sketchbook* published in 2005 with a slightly different take

---

3. A note on the use of pencils & watercolour: they became more widely used in the 18th and 19th centuries. J.R.R. Tolkien does not mention the use of watercolour in *The Lord of the Rings*, but there are two occurrences of the word "pencil". The first one is a comparison: "And standing there they surveyed the lands, for the morning was come; and they saw the towers of the City far below them like white pencils touched by the sunlight, and all the Vale of Anduin was like a garden, and the Mountains of Shadow were veiled in a golden mist" (*LotR*, 'The Steward and the King', 1007).

The second one hints at the use of this tool by an important character: "They found him all alone in his little room. It was littered with papers and pens and pencils; but Bilbo was sitting in a chair before a small bright fire" (*LotR*, 'Many Partings', 1022).

on the theme of the sketchbook. Lee, in his *Lord of the Rings Sketchbook* and his *Hobbit Sketchbook* (2019), presents his creative process in the making of the illustrations and the movie trilogies, whereas Howe lets his pictures hint at his thoughts and processes. Howe's writing in the book is mainly informational notices, as one would find in a touristic guide. Despite these two different approaches in the texts, the books clearly echo one another, offering similar layouts and an abundance of drawings on each spread.

The choice of pencil drawings over colour illustrations is not innocent. Howe's and Lee's books are sketchbooks rather than art books presenting their finished colour work. It means that to them, sketches and drawings are just as important as paintings. Pencils are the handiest tools to take on a trip and sketch along the way. They do not require water or thick paper. One can work from anywhere, on any papery surface. There is an immediacy with drawings that one does not really get with paint because of the time paint takes to dry.

Even though there are some colour illustrations in each of the three books, the mere number of pencil studies crystallizes the feeling that the two artists have travelled across Middle-earth and sketched as much as they could to show the marvels they have encountered on their way. These sketchbooks are the visual testimony the artists brought back from their own foray into the Secondary world.

In Lee's sketchbooks, there is a conflation of Middle-earth and New Zealand as he presents sketches created both for the illustrated editions of *The Lord of the Rings* and *The Hobbit*, and for the movie adaptations. When the artist presents the reader with variations on the theme of the Hobbit dwelling, one can interpret it as his trial and error process while looking for the perfect entrance to Bag End, but one can also easily imagine Lee walking around Hobbiton and taking notes, in sketches, of all the different dwellings he walked by. With Howe, there is a similar blend between New Zealand and Middle-earth, but it is not an aspect he dwells on in his writing, since his sketchbook works as a travel guide to the Secondary world.

Lee and Howe present themselves in their books as travellers, bringing back sketches from a place that only they can access bodily. Their journey is shrouded in mystery, but thanks to the wealth of sketches they share with the reader, one has a proper feeling of immersion, as if one stood behind them while they worked and peeked at their drawings in the making. This feeling relies heavily on the realism of their drawings and the way they blend together different inspirations taken from the Primary world to offer vistas that feel both familiar and foreign.

In their cases, sketches seem less like pencil explorations to find the one good way to depict their subject, than notes on the variations they observe of a specific theme. In this respect, their sketches are quite different from Tolkien's. Tolkien often wanted to draw a specific landscape, building, or city, and devoted several sketches to finding the correct way to depict it. For instance, he looked for the perfect angle and the right placement of elements in his sketches of Bag End. He did not draw a variety of Hobbit dwellings, but rather explored different ways to represent a specific one.

Artists as inhabitants of Middle-earth

Contrary to the artists as travellers coming back from the Secondary world, other artists imagine themselves as inhabitants of Middle-earth, practising their art with the techniques available to them in this imagined location and time.

This is the case of the Spanish artist Tómas Hijo, whose piece entitled "The Prancing Pony" received the 2016 Tolkien Society Award for Best Artwork. His Tolkien-related work is mainly composed of linocut prints. Hijo works first in pencil, then transfers his sketch onto a linoleum block to carve it before printing the design onto paper. The materials he uses are modern, but the technique of printing is centuries old. It could very well have been used in Middle-earth, either in the Victorianesque Shire, or in medieval-inspired cities like Minas Tirith.[4]

His technical process is a long one, but it enables him to print several identical copies of the same image in black and white. There is also a raised effect on the paper, because of the huge pressure applied to the piece. The paper has a slight relief where the lines of the block are printed, which is not something that can be achieved digitally.

Though his technique is very different from both Lee and Howe, Hijo also achieves a high degree of immersion, because of the level of details in his images. The pictures teem with dozens of small details that one can only see by getting close to the paper, so that the print fills one's whole vision and one feels transported into the Secondary world.

Many scenes take place at the same time in his "The Battle

---

4. The influence of the Middle Ages is also felt in the playfulness of Hijo's representations. Although the lines are kept simple because of the technique, all the characters embody a range of emotions and reactions. Some of them may evoke figures from German Expressionist prints, but one has to keep in mind that German Expressionist artists were inspired by medieval print-making and searched for a similar simplicity of means in their works.

of the Pelennor Fields"[5], but they do not come only from the homonym chapter. From "The Siege of Gondor", one can spot Denethor leading Faramir's bearers down the Silent Street. From "The Ride of the Rohirrim", the actual charge is represented in the top of the composition. One can even spot Éowyn and Merry. Further in the background, the ships of Umbar from the chapter "The Battle of the Pelennor Fields" are approaching.

In order to depict as many details as possible in one scene, Hijo opts for a bird's eye view.[6] The viewer is standing above the scene and looking down on it. The impression that one is diving into the picture is reinforced by the many vertical and diagonal lines in the composition, for instance the walls of Minas Tirith and the edge of the "pier of rock" (*LotR*, 'Minas Tirith', 782), dividing the city in half. The higher level of Minas Tirith is the one closest to the viewer and the ground level is the furthest away, but the diagonal movement invites the eye to go down and discover all the vignettes of action.

Last but not least, the eye is also guided by the colour palette. The elements closest to the viewer, or the ones the artist wants to draw attention to, are painted in contrasted tones. For instance, the opaque, light grey of the stone and the oliphaunt contrasts with the deep red of the tiled roofs, and the black lines. In comparison, the upper left-hand corner, where the colours are muted, attracts the eye less, so that the viewer's

---

5. See this print at: https://tomashijoart.bigcartel.com/product/the-battle-of-the-pelennor-fields-poster [accessed 15 March 2021].

6. The technical term for this specific type of perspective is "isometric projection": the three axes are foreshortened at the same degree. Many thanks to Denis Bridoux for pointing this out to me after my presentation at the online Tolkien Society Seminar.

gaze travels to this area of the image in a second time, after considering the rest.

With Hijo, immersion is two-fold: it comes both from the technique used, and from the way the artist composes his images. The overhead view he favours makes the viewer want to lean forward, not unlike a certain Hobbit gazing into the mirror of Galadriel and seeing a quick succession of events out of chronological order. Frodo's vision blends together big and small events just as the artist does in his depiction, in which a Nazgûl is juxtaposed with a stray cat.

Before Hijo, J.R.R. Tolkien himself also created examples of art from Middle-earth, for instance his *Númenórean Carpet* or the well-known leaves from the Book of Mazarbul. There would be much to say about Tolkien's designs from the Secondary world, and the importance of craftsmanship, which has been the subject of research papers in the past.[7] Let us simply note here the common thread weaving through Hijo's prints and some of Tolkien's drawings, which give an idea of art "from Middle-earth".

Hijo's prints achieve a very different type of immersion than Lee and Howe's sketches, but they all invite the viewers in. Hijo employs a technique that could have been in use in the Secondary world, whereas Lee and Howe take their contemporary tools to the imaginary world. Jay Johnstone embodies a third way, using historical techniques and iconography to create art inspired by Middle-earth through a Primary world's lens.

---

7. See for instance Hewitt, Gina L., "Handicraft, Hobbitcraft and the Fires of Mordor: The Arts and Crafts Movement, Industrial Revolution and The Lord of the Rings" (2014). *Master of Liberal Studies Theses*. 51<http://scholarship.rollins.edu/mls/51> [accessed 15 March 2021]. See also Denis Bridoux's various studies of Tolkien's "doodles".

Art in translation

Thomas Honegger, in his essay on Johnstone's *Isildur's Bane*,[8] shows through the analysis of this painting how the artist imagined "the work of a Middle-earth painter of the Third or Fourth Ages" (Honegger 2018, 2).[9]

Johnstone uses a visual language that is familiar to the viewer, in order to "translate" modes of representation from the Secondary world into the Primary world. His pictures work as comments, as they are not supposed to come from Middle-earth. Johnstone is aware that artists from the Secondary world would have different pictorial traditions, steeped into their own cultures. What he offers with his artworks are equivalents, in a pictorial language more familiar to viewers from our world. This approach mirrors that of Tolkien himself, who translated cultural references from Middle-earth world into cultural references specific to the Primary world, as he explains in Appendix F of *The Lord of the Rings* (*LotR*, Appendix F, II): the relation between the language of Rohan and the Common Speech was similar to that between Old English and Modern English, which is why Tolkien gave the Rohirrim names with Old English roots, although these names are not the ones in usage in Middle-earth.

Isildur's Bane and other pictures by Johnstone function similarly as analogies.[10] Through transposition and translation,

---

8. See this artwork here: https://jaystolkien.com/portfolio-items/isildurs-bane-gold-foil/ [accessed 15 March 2021].

9. This article was also reproduced in Johnstone's self-published art book *Tolkienography*.

10. ... which is ironic considering Tolkien's warnings against analogy when applied to his own works.

Johnstone creates art that blends together various artistic traditions to evoke the sense of a historical painting which does not come directly from Middle-earth but is an analogy of an artwork from the Secondary World.

Johnstone's portrait of *The High King Elessar*[11] evokes official representations of rulers or nobility from the 14th to the 16th centuries.[12] The inscription on the background was not a common feature at the time, but it appears for instance in a portrait of Jean II Le Bon, King of France,[13] or in a portrait of King Richard III.[14] In these historical portraits, the inscription is reduced to the minimum: the king's name and his function, which is even shortened in King Richard's portrait as "Ang. Rex" for the Latin "Angliae Rex", or "King of England". In Johnstone's portrait of King Elessar, the inscription details the subject's titles, his names and ancestry. It forms an impressive list that becomes almost decorative as it forms a lace-like pattern around the King's head. This mirrors the way Aragorn is referred to in the text, whether by himself or by heralds. On his coronation day, for instance, Faramir presents him as follows:

---

11. See this artwork here: https://jaystolkien.com/portfolio-items/the-high-king-elessar/ [accessed 15 March 2021].

12. Usually, the subject is painted in close-up (just the face and the neck are visible), in bust (the portrait shows the person up to the waist) or full-length. Here Johnstone makes the original choice of showing the character from his head to his knees, which was uncommon in historical portraits.

13. See this artwork here: https://www.louvre.fr/oeuvre-notices/jean-ii-le-bon-roi-de-france-1319-1364

14. See this artwork here: https://www.npg.org.uk/collections/search/portrait/mw05304/King-Richard-III

Here is Aragorn son of Arathorn, chieftain of the Dúnedain of Arnor, Captain of the Host of the West, bearer of the Star of the North, wielder of the Sword Reforged, victorious in battle, whose hands bring healing, the Elfstone, Elessar of the line of Valandil, Isildur's son, Elendil's son of Númenor (*LotR*, 'The Steward and the King', 1003).

A similar description is inscribed in calligraphy form in this painted portrait. In Johnstone's artworks, it looks as if characters from Middle-earth had escaped the pages and invaded the Primary World at various periods of time. King Elessar here is depicted as a medieval king in an official portrait.

Johnstone also studied illuminated manuscripts. To create his manuscript page *The King of the Golden Hall*,[15] he studied carefully the layout, iconography and techniques of manuscript artists from the Middle Ages. He then steeped Middle-earth iconography into these characteristics.[16] Hence, one can recognize here characters from *The Lord of the Rings* (Gandalf, the three hunters, Théoden, Éowyn and Gríma) as well as cultural symbols that pervade the text, such as the white tree and the crown, the horse on a green background, etc. The decorative frieze shaped like a tree in full bloom appears on both the historical page and Johnstone's recreation. His approach may be influenced by Pauline Baynes' faux-

15. See this artwork here: https://jaystolkien.com/portfolio-items/the-king-of-the-golden-hall-gold-foil/ [accessed 15 March 2021].

16. As Joel Merriner pointed out, this faux-medieval creation of Middle-earth iconography was also explored by Ukranian artist Sergei Iukhimov. See for instance: Merriner, Joel, "Intertextuality and Iconography in Sergei Iukhimov's Illustrations for The Lord of the Rings: Five Case Studies," *Journal of Tolkien Research:* Vol. 7 : Iss. 1 , Article 1 <https://scholar.valpo.edu/journaloftolkienresearch/vol7/iss1/1> [accessed 15 March 2021].

medieval illustrations for *Farmer Giles of Ham* (1949), in which the artist blended skillfully medieval iconography with intricate compositions and playful details, to the delight of Tolkien. Contrary to Baynes, Johnstone is not limited in terms of technique and reproduction (either black-and-white or two-colour illustrations in *Farmer Giles*), so he can fully explore medieval techniques and materials, including gold accents.

Lee also took inspiration from medieval manuscripts, as shows his illustration of *Bilbo in Rivendell*,[17] which borrows its window frame from the Limbourg Brothers' *Very Rich Hours of the Duke of Berry*.[18] In Lee's picture it is hard to define whether the top part of the image is decorative or architectural. It borrows motifs and colours from the manuscript to inject a sense of history into the illustration[19].

Medieval manuscripts find their way, in different forms, in pictures created by some of the artists considered here. This blend of the fictional with real-world inspirations adds another layer of history to an already historically rich world. It creates an interdependence between the two that was already suggested by the text, but is now reinforced in a visual way.

Tolkien himself took inspiration from existing historical periods and iconography in his sketches. For instance, the

17. See this watercolour here: http://tolkiengateway.net/wiki/File:Alan_ Lee_-_Bilbo_at_Rivendell.jpg [accessed 15 March 2021].
18. One exemplary illustration from this book of hours can be seen here: https://commons.wikimedia.org/wiki/File:Fr%C3%A8res_Limbourg_-_ Tr%C3%A8s_Riches_Heures_du_duc_de_Berry_-_mois_de_mai_-_ Google_Art_Project.jpg#/media/File:Frères_Limbourg_-_Très_Riches_ Heures_du_duc_de_Berry_-_mois_de_mai_-_Google_Art_Project.jpg [accessed 15 March 2021].
19. See Bretagnolle, Marie, 'Artists in Middle-earth: illustrating *The Lord of the Rings*', to be published in the Tolkien2019 proceedings.

crown he imagines for Gondor is inspired by Egyptian crowns. The author himself drew a parallel in his letters.

> I think the crown of Gondor (the S. Kingdom) was very tall, like that of Egypt, but with wings attached, not set straight back but at an angle. [Here is placed a small double sketch of the crown, seen in profile and from the front.] The N. Kingdom had only a *diadem* (III 323). Cf. the difference between the N. and S. kingdoms of Egypt (*Letters*, Letter 211, 281).

This is also a reminder that even though the Middle Ages are the most common source of inspiration for visual artists illustrating Tolkien's Middle-earth, there are many other areas of influence to consider.

Conclusion

All these artists echo Tolkien's often quoted letter 131 to Milton Waldman in which the author wished for "other minds and hands, wielding paint and music and drama" (145) to prolong his creation. Some of them have set out to offer the viewers art "from" Middle-earth rather than art "about" Middle-earth, as Hijo explained in his interview with the Tolkien Collector's Guide. The four artists presented here offer people of the 21st century an unprecedented visual tour of an invented world and the artworks that may have been created there. By doing so, they emphasise the impression of historical depth already provided by the legendarium, with its interlaced stories and mythical background.

Bibliography

Edmonds, Jeremy, *Artist Profile - Tómas Hijo*, forum post, Tolkien Collector's Guide, 6 June 2020 <https://www.tolkienguide.com/modules/newbb/viewtopic.php?topic_id=3715&forum=12&post_id=25543#forumpost25543> [accessed 9 January 2021].

Honegger, Thomas, 'Ut pictura tractatio' – Some Thoughts on Jay Johnstone's Isildur's Bane', 2018
<https://www.academia.edu/12234866/_Ut_pictura_tractatio_Some_Thoughts_on_Jay_Johnstone_s_Isildur_s_Bane_> [accessed 15 March 2021].

Howe, John, *Middle-Earth Traveller: Sketches from Bag End to Mordor*, (London: HarperCollins, 2018).

Lee, Alan, *The Lord of the Rings Sketchbook*, (London: HarperCollins, 2005).
— *The Hobbit Sketchbook*, (London: HarperCollins, 2019).

Tolkien, J.R.R., *The Letters of J.R.R. Tolkien*, ed. Humphrey Carpenter with the assistance of Christopher Tolkien (London: Allen & Unwin, 1981).
— *The Lord of the Rings*, illustrated by Alan Lee (London: HarperCollins, 1991).

Nazgûl Taller Than Night:
Tolkien and Speculative Realism

Nick Groom

This paper is an introduction to recent developments in philosophy and critical theory that may offer new directions in Tolkien studies. My aim is fourfold. First, to provide an introduction to the area of Speculative Realism. Secondly, to show how twenty-first-century approaches such these as can provide startling new readings of Tolkien. Thirdly, to outline how and why J.R.R. Tolkien's own writing has influenced these new critical approaches. And fourthly, to explain how Tolkien's writing might provide a perspective on the bigger conceptual and environmental concerns of the Anthropocene today.

I aim to cover these areas (if necessarily briefly) by examining the representation and significance of darkness in the opening chapters of *The Lord of the Rings*. As I have already argued elsewhere (Groom 2014, 298-9), Tolkien's depiction of darkness draws on earlier literary and cultural representations, but, from the perspective of the twenty-first century, the idea of darkness is also enmeshed with the weird and the eerie – terms that have become evocative touchstones in recent philosophical and critical thinking. There is effectively a "spectrum" of philosophical darkness, from the neo-Platonic writings of Dionysius the Areopagite (or "Pseudo-Dionysius") in late Antiquity to the medieval Christian theology of *The*

Cloud of Unknowing to what the radical philosopher Eugene Thacker today calls 'Black Illumination' (Thacker 2015, 126-31).

Dionysius the Areopagite's treatise *Mystical Theology*, written in the sixth-century, begins with the promise that it will lead us to

> the super-unknown and super-brilliant and highest summit of the mystic Oracles, where the simple and absolute and changeless mysteries of theology lie hidden within the super-luminous gloom of the silence, revealing hidden things, which in its deepest darkness shines above the most super-brilliant, and in the altogether impalpable and invisible, fills to overflowing the eyeless minds with glories of passing beauty. (Dionysius the Areopagite, Caput I, section I, 130)[1]

Over 800 years later these ideas were taken up in the late-fourteenth-century in the anonymous *The Cloud of Unknowing* – Tolkien had at least two editions of this text and through the Early English Text Society also worked with Phyllis Hodgson, who edited of *The Cloud of Unknowing* in 1944 (Cilli 2019, xxviii, 11, 355; Hammond and Scull 2017, 412). *The Cloud of Unknowing* draws heavily on Dionysius the Areopagite, and its partner text *Epistle of Privy Counsel* quotes his advice, "That meek darkness be thy mirror". As the Anglican mystic Evelyn Underhill explained in her edition (a noticeably more archaic translation than Hodgson's lean version):

I would like to thank Will Sherwood and the Tolkien Society for providing the opportunity to deliver this paper, and Dr Henry Bartholomew for his helpful comments on the text.

1. In this essay, where relevant I quote from editions with which Tolkien was likely to have been familiar.

What is this darkness? It is the "night of the intellect" into which we are plunged when we attain to a state of consciousness which is above thought; enter on a plane of spiritual experience with which the intellect cannot deal. This is the "Divine Darkness" – the Cloud of Unknowing, or of Ignorance, "dark with excess of light" – preached by Dionysius the Areopagite.... It is "a dark mist ... which seemeth to be between thee and the light thou aspirest to". (*Book Of Contemplation* 1922, 30)[2]

So darkness is a positive state here – a condition of being beyond the known and knowable world, and so closer to God.

But of course through works such as John Milton's *Paradise Lost* (1667) and Edmund Burke's *Philosophical Enquiry into the Origin of Our Ideas of the Sublime and Beautiful* (1757), darkness has also traditionally had terrifying and annihilating qualities, and so the state simultaneously represents both the highest spiritual insight and the most profound threat to one's humanity (Cilli 2019, 196-7, 36, 130). Darkness is symbolic of the opaque: the world hidden from us, beyond our comprehension – and this questions what we are doing here at all, so it is a potentially nihilistic way of thinking. And in recent philosophy, this has fed into works such as Graham Harman's *Weird Realism* (2012), Eugene Thacker's three-volume *The Horror of Philosophy* (2010-15), and the late Mark Fisher's *The Weird and the Eerie* (2016). These thinkers are all concerned

2. Evelyn Underhill was a pioneering divine with strong Roman Catholic sympathies, and the author of the highly influential volume Mysticism: *A Study of the Nature and Development of Man's Spiritual Consciousness* (1911); she was also the first non-academic woman to lecture on religion at the University of Oxford (1921-22; Tolkien was at Leeds at the time). Underhill was a renowned intellectual, knew Charles Williams, and corresponded with C.S. Lewis after the publication of *Out of the Silent Planet* (1938). Her surname is obviously suggestive to readers of Tolkien.

with what cannot be explained or rationalized.

Now, to explain Speculative Realism (a.k.a. Object-Oriented Ontology) in a short paper is rather ambitious, but I will begin with two models suggested by Harman, before adding various comments by Thacker and Fisher. Harman suggests a thought experiment. Imagine a lump of plutonium in the desert. Pretty quickly it kills off all plant and animal life nearby, and makes the sand radioactive. But importantly, the plutonium also *retains* the potential to act: the ability to kill any living thing (including humans) that may approach it in the future. At the level of common sense, this is obvious – plutonium is a dangerous material – but at a philosophical level, this is fascinating: how can plutonium be categorized? So, according to Harman, in the plutonium "there is an *additional reality*" [my italics] to its current context. But it is too easy way to explain this as a "potential" to affect living things: "What is weak about this approach", says Harman, "is that the theme of potential allows us a sneaky way to evade the difficult question of what the *actuality* of the lethal quality is". Its possible future effects are unknown – "yet to be determined" – but are nevertheless real: they are undecided but actual (Harman 2010, 103-4).

The big conceptual leap here is that "It remains unclear just what objects are, but it is already clear that they far exceed the human-centered" (Harman 2010, 116). So this is a way to think about objects rather than humans as being at the centre of reality. And what are objects? Harman claims that, "'Object' can refer to trees, atoms, and songs, and also to armies, banks, sports franchises, and fictional characters" (Harman 2010, 147). Donald Trump is no more or less an object than is a vampire or a pillar of salt or the internet (Harman 2010, 163).

This is certainly worth considering: there is a hint here of a world that is governed by objects which we as humans cannot understand – or even define – but which nevertheless have continuous and the most profound effects on us. Readers may now be thinking of the One Ring, but for this short paper I have chosen a slightly more manageable example. But before introducing it, I will outline another aspect of Harman's thinking from his book on the horror writer H.P. Lovecraft – Lovecraft's Cthulhu mythos being predicated on the idea that humans are incidental to the universe, and that reality is in fact organized around monstrous inter-dimensional creatures from outer space that occasionally appear on Earth.

For Harman, "No other writer is so perplexed by the gap between objects and the power of language to describe them, or between objects and the qualities they possess", arguing that Lovecraft is effectively a "cubist" in literature (Harman 2012, 3). He argues that "Lovecraft's major gift as a writer is his deliberate and skilful obstruction of all attempts to paraphrase him" (Harman 2012, 9): he calls this *"weird realism"*, and spends much of the book analyzing passages from Lovecraft to demonstrate and develop this idea. Rather than follow Harman, however, I think that there is a much better example of these issues of language in M.R. James, the English writer of ghost stories – not least because Tolkien cited James's books *Ghost-Stories of an Antiquary* (1904) in a version of 'On Fairy-Stories' (Cilli 2019, 132; *OFS*, 261).[3]

---

3. Tolkien possessed the anthology *Swords and Sorcery* which includes Lovecraft's tale 'The Doom That Came to Sarnath'; however as the book was published in 1963 and sent to Tolkien by the editor L. Sprague de Camp in 1964 it obviously post-dates *LotR* (Cilli 2019, 68; Hammond and Scull 2017, 412). Dale Nelson suggests that James McBryde's illustration to James's tale 'Canon Alberic's Scrapbook' may have influenced Tolkien's portrayal of Gollum (*Beyond Bree*, November 2008 and January 2009): see Stride 2017).

In 'Canon Alberic's Scrapbook', James describes an illustration of a hideous figure: "Imagine one of the awful bird-catching spiders of South America translated into human form, and endowed with intelligence just less than human, and you will have some faint conception of the terror inspired by the appalling effigy" (James 1904, 18-19). It would plainly be preposterous to paraphrase this as follows: "If you think of a dim-witted man crossed with a tarantula spider, that really won't frighten you as much as this picture would"(!). The effect of James's sentence is not simply in its use of vocabulary, which fluctuates between apparent precision and despairing imprecision, but his reluctance – or inability – to speak of the unutterable. In Harman's terms, such language fails, because this "reality ... eludes all literal speech" (Harman 2012, 54; also 234-5).

At the same time that Harman was developing his ideas, another philosopher – the fashionable Eugene Thacker – was on a similar track, comparing "the language of darkness mysticism or negative theology" of earlier eras (such as the writings of Dionysius the Areopagite and *The Cloud of Knowing*) with the supernatural horror literature of the past 200 years (Thacker 2011, 2). It is an audacious move: for Thacker, "Horror is about the paradoxical thought of the unthinkable" – and he makes these "blind spots" his central concern: the world is "superlatively beyond human comprehension" (Thacker 2011, 9). Hence in *Tentacles Longer Than Night* (2015) – from which I take my own title – Thacker proposes "mis-reading works of horror as if they were works of philosophy", arguing that Edgar Allan Poe, Lovecraft, and their ilk are philosophers, and that their horror writing is "essentially idea-driven, rather than plot-driven" (Thacker 2015, 11). Now, we all know that Tolkien argued that his Middle-earth writings were in one sense simply

43

the necessary background to his primary creation, the Elvish languages – but is it also possible to (mis-) read Tolkien as driven by philosophical ideas?

Thacker discusses both Dionysius the Areopagite and the occultist Cornelius Agrippa's *De Occulta Philosophia* (1533) to develop the idea that the world is hidden, or "occulted" – early meanings of "occult" being "hidden from sight; concealed.... A hidden or secret thing" (OED).[4] This "occulted world" therefore "makes its presence known to us and yet in doing so reveals the unknown". So what is revealed is "the 'hiddenness' of the world" – and this potentially leads to the anti-humanism and nihilism that, for some, characterizes Speculative Realism – "a blank, anonymous world that is indifferent to human knowledge, much less to our all-too-human wants and desires" (Thacker 2015, 52-4). However, this thinking can also offer a radical way of making sense of our current environmental crisis, as I will suggest in the conclusion to this paper. But in any case, what I think characterizes these philosophical approaches is an overwhelming sense of *presence*, which distinguishes them from the predominantly linguistic turn of continental philosophy of a generation ago (although even that movement was ultimately haunted by spectral figures). There is a teeming attendance in OOO (Object-Oriented Ontology) – loads of stuff everywhere all the time – which persistently exposes the limitations of human comprehension and perspectives.

Finally, the late philosopher Mark Fisher (d. 2017) moves the discussion into the "weird" and the "eerie", again using Lovecraft:

---

4. "Fooles know, it's not words, or expressions, or oculars define, but things, natures, intentions, intrinsiques, and occults" (S.H., *Knaves and Fooles in Folio* (London, 1648), fol. 5).

What the weird and the eerie have in common is a preoccupation with the strange. The strange – not the horrific…. a fascination for the outside, for that which lies beyond standard perception, cognition and experience. (Fisher 2016, 8)

He defines the *weird* as "constituted by a presence", whereas the *eerie* "occurs either when there is something present where there should be nothing, or there is nothing present when there should be something" (Fisher 2016, 61). And both of these are distinct from the "uncanny" (Fisher 2016, 9; see Bartholomew 2019, 357-83). Fisher offers the particularly arresting example of stone circles:

stone circles confront us with a symbolic structure that has entirely rotted away, so that the deep past of humanity is revealed to be in effect an illegible alien civilisation, its rituals and modes of subjectivity unknown to us. (Fisher 2016, 89-90)

While a discussion of the Barrow-Downs is beyond the scope of this paper, this is nevertheless expressive enough as it stands: the past is not simply a foreign country; it is an alien planet.[5]

Tolkien certainly helped to shift popular perceptions of the human in the second half of the twentieth century by sidelining human agency in his works, which is why he may be considered an unlikely forebear of Speculative Realism. There are very few recognizable human characters in Middle-

---

5. See my essay, "'The Ghostly Language of the Ancient Earth": Tolkien, Geology, and Romantic Lithology', *The Romantic Spirit in the Works of J. R. R. Tolkien*, ed. Julian Eilmann and Will Sherwood (Zurich: Walking Tree, forthcoming).

Earth – Aragorn and Boromir are both descended from Númenóreans so are of a mightier stamp than everyday folk (and Aragorn living to the immense age of 210). In fact, the most relatable human characters in *LotR* are perhaps Barliman Butterbur, Beregond (the guardsman of Gondor who initiates Peregrin), and the dead Haradrim pondered by Sam, as well as the Rohirrim more generally, while there are no humans at all in *The Hobbit* until Thorin and Co. arrive in Laketown.[6] The focus in both books is, of course, on Hobbits, with whom readers nevertheless readily identify. Hobbits are certainly "humane" – the original, now obsolete, meaning of the word being "civil, courteous, or obliging towards others" (*OED*) – but Tolkien repeatedly stresses their physical differences, their cultural differences, and their social and political differences when compared with the Race of Men. Hobbits are no more than four and a half feet high (itself exceptional), yet have extraordinary stamina and resilience; there is little high culture at all in The Shire, and popular culture is focused on food, gardening, singing and dancing, and oral story-telling; and there is no internecine conflict in Hobbit society (even during 'The Scouring of the Shire'), little technological progress, and absolutely no colonial ambitions or commercial aspirations. Likewise, Dwarves are not human, still less the immortal Elves, and Orcs meanwhile are comprehensively demonized by nearly everyone – interestingly, it is only the Hobbits who get a glimpse of Orc culture and society.

So Tolkien helped to normalize the non-anthropocentric (human-centred) narrative, which had already been developing in works from Anna Sewell's *Black Beauty* (1877) to George

---

6. I discount Beorn as he is a skin-changer.

Orwell's *Animal Farm* (1945). But in *LotR*, Tolkien was neither writing a children's book nor a political allegory. Rather, and the range and complexity of non-anthropocentric characters in addition to the somewhat restrained supernatural elements (such as the Ringwraiths), mysterious and unexplained figures (such as Tom Bombadil and Goldberry), and especially an emphasis on apparently inanimate objects and places that demonstrate agency and identity (the One Ring, the Palantíri, the Old Forest) makes the novel particularly rewarding from a Speculative Realist perspective. As the Elf Gildor observes to the Hobbits, decentring them from their homeland, "it is not your own Shire.... Others dwelt here before hobbits were; and others will dwell here again when hobbits are no more" (*FR*, 'Three is Company', 120).

But in the last part of this paper I'll address darkness. Darkness pervades Tolkien's writing. In *LotR* the darkness is already gathering in the first chapter. Bilbo departs in the dark; Gandalf "staring after him into the darkness" and then "sitting in the dark" (*FR*, 'A Long-Expected Party', 59). In the chapter 'The Shadow of the Past' Gandalf tells Frodo of the Ring inscribed with the words "*in the darkness bind them*", and within moments Frodo is aware that "Fear seemed to stretch out a vast hand, like a dark cloud rising in the East and looming up to engulf him" (*FR*, 77). Similarly, while at Buckland Frodo dreams that "He was on a dark heath" (*FR*, 'A Conspiracy Unmasked', 151). By the end of the novel, Frodo is haunted by a sense of menace articulated by Thacker: "What if 'horror' has less to do with a fear of death and more to do with the dread of life?" (Thacker 2011, 98).

It is with the arrival of the Ringwraiths, though, that darkness acquires agency. The first Black Rider the Hobbits encounter on the road disturbs the conventional senses – an invisible face that is seemingly trying to hear, trying to smell:

> The riding figure sat quite still with its head bowed, *as if* listening. From inside the hood came a noise *as if* of someone sniffing to catch an elusive scent; the head turned from side to side of the road. (*FR*, 'Three is Company', 109, my italics)

Within just five pages there is an uncanny repetition of the scene, the disturbance deepened in a flicker of animated opacity:

> It looked like the black shade of a horse led by a smaller black shadow. The black shadow stood close to the point where they had left the path, and it swayed from side to side. Frodo thought he heard the sound of snuffling. The shadow bent to the ground, and then began to crawl towards him. (*FR*, 'Three is Company', 113)

There is certainly something *weird* about this: a presence that is both indeterminate and strangely wrong – what Thacker, writing on Lovecraft, calls "blasphemous life": "*Blasphemous life is the life that is living but that should not be living*" (Thacker 2011, 104). Similarly, as the Hobbits cross the Brandywine River on the Buckleberry Ferry,

> On the far stage, under the distant lamps, they could just make out a figure: it looked like a dark black bundle left behind. But as they looked it seemed to move and sway this way and that, as if searching the ground. It then crawled, or went crouching, back into the gloom beyond the lamps. (*FR*, 'A Conspiracy Unmasked', 140)

It/they seem to look like inanimate shapes yet snuffle and sway and crawl – or crouch – which is it?

It is Strider who explains the Black Riders as living in an "occulted world":

> They themselves do not see the world of light as we do, but our shapes cast shadows in their minds, which only the noon sun destroys; and in the dark they perceive many signs and forms that are hidden from us: then they are most to be feared. And at all times they smell the blood of living things, desiring and hating it. Senses, too, there are other than sight or smell. We can feel their presence ... they feel ours more keenly. (*FR*, 'A Knife in the Dark', 255)

And their horses are their eyes in this sightless existence.

When Frodo confronts the Nazgûl on Weathertop, where the word "shadow" is persistently stressed, "So black were they that they seemed like black holes in the deep shade behind them" (*FR*, 'A Knife in the Dark', 261). But Frodo, wearing the Ring, sees them in another way, "beneath their black wrappings" – and they are skeletal white and spectral grey, and now their eyes are weaponized: "Their eyes fell on him and pierced him" (*FR*, 262). Frodo is changed after being wounded: his senses are more acute, and his night vision keener – he is more accommodated to the dark.

These depictions of the Ringwraiths seem to me to draw not so much on Lovecraft's bizarre, inter-dimensional monsters as on the unnervingly undefined shapes of horror in the tales of M.R. James, which are both tangible and phantasmic – like the ghosts of mediaeval folklore. Tolkien quoted from James's first two collections of ghost stories, which include several such figures. In 'The Mezzotint', for instance, "In the middle of the lawn in front of the unknown house there was a figure.... It was crawling on all fours towards the house, and it was muffled in a strange black garment with a cross on its back" (James 1904, 65). There is a later glimpse of the figure, again a mix of accuracy, hesitancy, and the inexpressible:

> The moon was behind it, and the black drapery hung down over its face so that only hints of that could be seen, and what was visible made the spectators profoundly thankful that they could see no more than a white dome-like forehead and a few straggling hairs.... the legs of the appearance alone could be plainly discerned, and they were horribly thin. (James 1904, 75)[7]

Most strikingly, perhaps, in "'Oh, Whistle, and I'll Come to You, My Lad'", Professor Parkins is attacked in his bedroom in the inn in which he is staying – much as the Hobbits risk being attacked at the Prancing Pony:

> It stood for the moment in a band of dark shadow, and he had not seen what its face was like. Now it began to move, in a stooping posture, and all at once the spectator realized, with some horror and some relief, that it must be blind, for it seemed to feel about it with its muffled arms in a groping and random fashion. (James 1904, 222)

Admittedly the being does move with supernatural speed, but when Parkins alerts the Colonel who rushes in, all there

7. Like other Jamesian horrors this creature could also have influenced the depiction of Gollum (see above, note 3).

was "before him on the floor lay a tumbled heap of bed-clothes" (James 1904, 223). The being's blindness and speed suggests that it has other sensory powers.

These passages try to express an unspeakable reality through, respectively, a haunted engraving and an accidental and inexplicable summoning. This language is not the vertiginous prose of Lovecraft, but shifts between the weird and the eerie, between what is perhaps there and what is perhaps not there, between apparent presences and absences – and all framed by doubt that any of this is really happening. The prose is unsettling as it glimpses other, hidden realities – "occulted worlds" – that human language struggles to represent.

So, what is reality? What would you see beyond the phenomenal? Nothing? Or wonder? Or something incomprehensibly terrifying. Unlike the "cosmic pessimism" of much Speculative Realism, Tolkien is able to suggest that all three are possible. Yes, the darkness is threatening: as Gandalf says in Rivendell, "We are sitting in a fortress. Outside it is getting dark" (*FR*, 'Many Meetings', 296). But darkness is also woven into Tinúviel's hair in the lay sung by Strider – "*her hair like shadow following*" (*FR*, 'A Knife in the Dark', 257) – and the Hobbits in particular use darkness to their advantage. Moreover, the darkness of the Old Forest is of a different order than that of the Ringwraiths – and seems inimical to them – as is that on the Barrow-Downs where, similarly mixed with mist and fog, the dark seems to generate a specifically linguistic bewilderment of incantations and chants.

Speculative Realism can, then, be defined as *realist* in that it rejects earlier philosophy that is based on experiences and perceptions solely as "appearances that exist in the mind of human perceivers", as this ultimately separates us from the reality of things in themselves (Rohlf 2020).[8] Speculative Realists argue that this sort of Kantian philosophy has little interest in the inanimate world in which we live – although philosophers in this tradition can still die from exposure to plutonium, drown in the sea, fall from mountain tops, and so forth. The word *speculative* is used to indicate that beyond common-sense apprehension there is "a darker form of 'weird realism' bearing little resemblance to the presuppositions of everyday life" – all that is hidden, the dark matter (Harman 2010, 2).[9] Hence the fascination in Speculative Realism for Cthulhu, and horror in general, and perhaps a way to think about Tolkien.

Nevertheless, Tolkien offers a far more optimistic direction for Speculative Realism than that entangled with horror. Not only can Tolkien's figures of darkness be reworked into forms of resistance and liberty and ontological ascent, but this sudden shift of perspective or fortunes characterizes his coinage "eucatastrophe". Tolkien identified eucatastrophe in both fairy stories and the Gospels and defined it as "the sudden happy turn in a story which pierces you with a joy that brings tears" (*Letters*, Letter 89, 100; *OFS* 75, 119). Hence, Strider is first encountered enveloped in shadow (his own hidden identity) and walks the Paths of the Dead before succeeding to the throne as Elessar. Frodo likewise feels his way through what in *The Cloud of*

8. According to Harman, "these [Speculative Realist] philosophies all reject the central teaching of [Immanuel] Kant's Copernican Revolution, which turns philosophy into a meditation on human finitude and forbids it from discussing reality in itself" (Harman 2010, 2).
9. Philosophically, for Harman: "Reality is partly objective and partly perspectival. It is partly real, partly of a narrative character, and partly the effect of political displacements" (Harman 2010, 79).

Unknowing is described as the "dark mist" of his mind, eluding capture as he and Sam hide in disguise among the shadows of Mordor; Frodo stumbles on, stripped of his identity as he approaches "the end of all things" (*RK*, 'Mount Doom', 271; 'The Field of Cormallen', 275). "No taste of food, no feel of water, no sound of wind, no memory of tree or grass or flower, no image of moon or star are left to me. I am naked in the dark" (*RK*, 'Mount Doom', 258). He is about to be transformed into song, into myth, into wonder, and on the return journey this newly emerging transcendent state of being is evident in the silent exchanges between Gandalf and the Elves:

> Often ... they would sit together under the stars, recalling the ages that were gone and all their joys and labours in the world, or holding council, concerning the days to come. If any wanderer had chanced to pass, little would he have seen or heard, and it would have seemed to him only that he saw grey figures, carved in stone, memorials of forgotten things now lost in unpeopled lands. For they did not move or speak with mouth, looking from mind to mind; and only their shining eyes stirred and kindled as their thoughts went to and fro. (*RK*, 'Many Partings', 319-20)

This is the "hidden silence" expressed by Pseudo-Dionysius – not despair, but fulfilment (Corrigan and Harrington 2019).

So it is that Frodo's final journey – like so many of his others – is through the night. For him, there is now the hallowed peace of Valinor through the darkness of Middle-Earth:

> and the sails were drawn up, and the wind blew, and slowly the ship slipped away down the long grey firth; and the light of the glass of Galadriel that Frodo bore glimmered and was lost.

And the ship went out into the High Sea and passed on into the West, until at last on a night of rain Frodo smelled a sweet fragrance on the air and heard the sound of singing that came over the water. And then it seemed to him that as in his dream in the house of Bombadil, the grey rain-curtain turned all to silver glass and was rolled back, and he beheld white shores and beyond them a far green country under a swift sunrise. (*RK*, 'The Grey Havens', 378)

Conclusion

How might any of this provide a perspective on the wider concerns of the Anthropocene – our current predicament of catastrophic human intervention in the environment that has caused climate change and global pandemic?[10] Middle-earth itself is a mysterious and perilous realm, often inimical to sentient life, and with secrets deeper than the Dwarves delved in Moria. The Old Forest is a telling example of antagonistic ecology – aggressive to the point that the Hobbits burnt down many of its trees, and still bearing unfathomable arboreal grudges. It is not a sentimentalized pastoral for tree-huggers: it is a hallucinatory, weird, and lethal landscape – like Harman's thought experiment with plutonium, the Old Forest has "an additional reality" to that perceived by the Hobbits. And yet it can nevertheless be navigated through song. In our own current obscurity the creative imagination, challenged by the all-too-real threats of the twenty-first century, remains our best – and perhaps ultimately our only – hope. *The Lord of the Rings* both exemplifies and advocates such inspired artistry, such magic, and such song (De Lucia 2020, 339; Curry 2019, 12-13).

---

10. And so I await Covid-19 readings of Tolkien with interest.

Bibliography

Agamben, Giorgio, *Homo Sacer: Sovereign Power and Bare Life*, (Stanford: Stanford University Press, 1998).

[Anon.], *A Book Of Contemplation the which is called The Cloud Of Unknowing, in the which a Soul is Oned with God*, ed. and trans. Evelyn Underhill, 2nd edn (London: John M. Watkins, 1922).

[Anon.], *The Cloud of Unknowing and The Book of Privy Counseling*, ed. and trans. Phyllis Hodgson (Oxford: Early English Text Society, 1944), repr. ed. William Johnston (New York: Image Books, 1973).

Bartholomew, H.G., 'Enstranged Strangers: OOO, the Uncanny, and the Gothic', *Open Philosophy* 2 (2019), 357-83.

Cilli, Oronzo, *Tolkien's Library: An Annotated Checklist*, (Edinburgh: Luna Press Publishing, 2019).

Corrigan, Kevin and L. Michael Harrington, 'Pseudo-Dionysius the Areopagite', 30 April 2019, *The Stanford Dictionary of Philosophy* (2018 online edn) <https://plato.stanford.edu/entries/pseudo-dionysius-areopagite/> [accessed 25 March 2021].

Curry, Patrick, *Enchantment: Wonder in Modern Life*, (Edinburgh: Floris Books, 2019).

De Lucia, Vito, 'Rethinking the Encounter Between Law and Nature in the Anthropocene: From Biopolitical Sovereignty to Wonder', *Law and Critique* 31 (2020), 329-49.

"Dionysius the Areopagite" ["Pseudo-Dionysius"], *Mystic Theology*, in *The Works of Dionysius the Areopagite. Part I. Divine Names, Mystic Theology, Letters, &c.*, trans. John Parker (London: James Parker and Co., 1897 [vol. 2 pub. 1899]), 129-37.

Fisher, Mark, *The Weird and the Eerie*, (London: Repeater Books, 2016).

Groom, Nick, 'The English Literary Tradition: Shakespeare to the Gothic', *A Companion to J.R.R. Tolkien*, ed. Stuart Lee (Oxford: Blackwell, 2014), 286-302.

Hammond, Wayne G. and Christina Scull, *The J.R.R. Tolkien Companion and Guide: Chronology*, rev. edn (London: HarperCollins, 2017).

Harman, Graham, 'Bruno Latour, King of Networks' [1999], *Towards Speculative Realism: Essays and Lectures* (Winchester and Washington: Zero Books, 2010), 67-92.
— 'Object-Oriented Philosophy' [1999], *Towards Speculative Realism: Essays and Lectures* (Winchester and Washington: Zero Books, 2010), 93-104.
— 'The Revival of Metaphysics in Continental Philosophy' [2002], *Towards Speculative Realism: Essays and Lectures* (Winchester and Washington: Zero Books, 2010), 105-21.
— 'Space, Time, and Essence: An Object-Oriented Approach' [2008], *Towards Speculative Realism: Essays and Lectures* (Winchester and Washington: Zero Books, 2010), 140-69.
— 'Preface' [2009], *Towards Speculative Realism: Essays and Lectures* (Winchester and Washington: Zero Books, 2010), 1-3.

— *Weird Realism: Lovecraft and Philosophy*, (Winchester and Washington: Zero Books, 2012).

M.R. James, *Ghost-Stories of an Antiquary*, (London: Edward Arnold, 1904).

Rohlf, Michael, 'Immanuel Kant', 28 July 2020, *The Stanford Dictionary of Philosophy* (2018 online edn) <https://plato.stanford.edu/entries/kant/> [accessed 25 March 2021].

Stride, Daniel, 'Cosmic Horror and Tolkien', 4 January 2017 <https://phuulishfellow.wordpress.com/2017/01/04/cosmic-horror-and-tolkien/> [accessed 25 March 2021].

Thacker, Eugene, *In The Dust of This Planet, [Horror of Philosophy, vol. 1]* (Winchester and Washington: Zero Books, 2011).
— *Tentacles Longer Than Night, [Horror of Philosophy, vol. 3]* (Winchester and Washington: Zero Books, 2015).
— *Cosmic Pessimism*, (Minneapolis: University of Minnesota Press, 2015).

Tolkien, J.R.R., *The Lord of the Rings*, (London, Boston, and Sydney: George Allen & Unwin, 1979).
— *The Letters of J.R.R. Tolkien*, ed. by Humphrey Carpenter with the assistance of Christopher Tolkien (London, Boston, and Sydney: George Allen & Unwin, 1981).
— *On Fairy-Stories*, ed. by Verlyn Flieger and Douglas A. Anderson (London: HarperCollins, 2008).

Tolkien's Grave as a Site of Memory

Mina D. Lukić
and
Dejan M. Vukelić

The following paper aims to address Tolkien's grave as a multi-layered site of memory. First, the regular functions of funerary monuments are discussed and put into perspective of cultural memory studies. The role of epitaphs is analysed, as well as the practice of visiting famous authors' graves developed during the 19th century, and very much alive today. Second, Tolkien's own epitaph is considered as his personal statement and a testimony to his desire to set in stone the connection between his marriage and the story of Beren and Lúthien. Special attention is then given to the current reception and memory practices related to Tolkien's final resting place, stressing its distinctive role as a pilgrimage site. Third, the results of a survey conducted among Tolkien fans in January 2021 are examined to ascertain what visiting the grave meant for them, as well as illustrate their attitudes towards the site, the epitaph, and their understanding of the messages the monument conveys. Finally, in addition to individual, private visits and acts of remembrance, the ceremony of Enyalië, the final stage of Oxonmoot, is considered as an organised commemorative act which adds new layers of meaning and enhances the mnemonic capacity of Tolkien's grave as a site of memory.

Grave as a Site of Memory

The concept of *site of memory* (fr. *lieux de mémoire*) was first introduced by French historian Pierre Nora who defined it as "any significant entity, whether material or non-material in nature, which by dint of human will or the work of time has become a symbolic element of the memorial heritage of any community" (Nora 1996, xvii). It does not only refer to public monuments and places that embody cultural memory and a sense of historical continuity in strictly spatial terms, but it likewise relates to mnemonic practices such as festivals, holidays and anniversaries. It is in this light that Tolkien's grave and commemorative activities around it are analysed.

Nora paid special attention to sanctuaries, mausoleums, museums, archives, graveyards and cemeteries, denoting these sites of memory as the boundary stones of another age or "illusions of eternity" (Nora 1996, 6). In this regard, his position is close to Michel Foucault's concept of *heterotopias*, or other places – *other* in relation to ordinary or everyday cultural spaces. A cemetery is a highly heterotopian place whose *otherness* stems from *its specific* logic: it "begins with this strange heterochronism [inversion of time], that, for the individual, is the loss of life, and with this quasi-eternity in which he incessantly dissolves and fades away" (Foucault 2008, 20). Paradoxically, at the time of death, the mnemonic potential of final resting places become linked with physical presence of the deceased, whilst simultaneously denoting their absence. Associations with the macabre and somber feelings of transience of human existence on one hand, and, on the other, belief in the afterlife and the immortality of the human soul, is precisely what gives cemeteries their sacredness and brings a sense of awe to the visitors. As Toussaint and Decrop (2013, 15–21) point out, a cemetery's sacred character is often confirmed through gift-giving, myths, rituals and other ways of marking the sacred environment, thus providing visitors an opportunity to develop a deeper emotional and spiritual connection with their dear ones or with certain renowned figures whose ideas, beliefs, and value systems they strive to be associated with.

Since the dawn of time, graves have been the oldest form of remembering. However, in Europe, it was not until the 14th century that a greater concern over the choice of the burial place came to the fore, and it wasn't until the 19th Century that churchyards became the dominant places of burial. This started changing from the end of the 18th and beginning of the 19th century, when modern cemeteries were established as new places of burial, and when paying melancholic visits to the graves of the beloved ones, in a way familiar to us nowadays, became common practice (Ariès 1976, 69). Paired with a decline of religiosity during this period, this practice is well described by the renowned French medievalist Philippe Ariès, who noticed that "those who no longer go to church still go to the cemetery, where they have become accustomed to place flowers on the tombs. They meditate there, that is to say they evoke the dead person and cultivate his memory" (1976, 72–3).

At the same time, visiting historic cemeteries and resting places of notable individuals became popular and developed into a mass phenomenon when it came to writers. Great literature became a sort of "substitute for religious beliefs", as Matthew Arnold put it,[1] being regarded as a means of self-discovery,

---

1. See James C. Livingston, *Matthew Arnold and Christianity: His Religious Prose Writings* (1986).

frequently leading to adoration and immense popularity of writers. The desire to get closer to the authors who had such a formative effect on readers' lives motivated people to pay them homage by visiting the places where they were born, lived, or died. This produced a figure of *the literary tourist*[2] whose travels are frequently described as pilgrimage-like.

Visiting places like Westminster Abbey, Père-Lachaise Cemetery in Paris, or Moscow's Novodevichy Cemetery has remained a source of inspiration and social interaction to the present day, and famous people's graves rank high on the list of tourist attractions (Seaton 2002; Seaton 2019, 66–8; Pliberšek et al. 2019, 76–9). However, some forms of expressing love and gratitude in the era of mass tourism may be disrespectful, desecrating or even damaging to the grave of the person venerated, as in the case of lipstick kisses on Oscar Wilde's tomb in Père-Lachaise cemetery, where a glass barrier was introduced in 2011 in order to protect the monument from further decay caused by cleaning.

Ariès argued extensively on death rites, highlighting the significance of epitaphs on tombstones and their role in preserving the identity of the deceased. The inscriptions on gravestones represent an indispensable component of memorisation: they assert the identity of the departed (names, years of birth and death) and in many cases provide some additional information about their life, status, profession, beliefs, and similar, as something which needs to be considered and remembered. From the 17th Century onwards commemorative inscriptions have become

2. See Samantha Matthews' *Poetical Remains: Poets' Graves, Bodies, and Books in the Nineteenth Century* (2004), and Nicola Watson's *The Literary Tourist: Readers and Places in Romantic and Victorian Britain* (2006) and *Literary Tourism and Nineteenth-Century Culture* (2009).

such an important element in funeral culture to the extent that they often surpassed the very monument itself in importance, arousing strong impressions in visitors (Ariès 1976, 69).

Most of the inscriptions are brief and formal, usually containing a record of the name, age, title, and occupation, but they can also contain quotes, verses, and credos, which gain additional significance on famous authors' gravestones. Some epitaphs reflect the writer's love of home and birthplace, such as H.P. Lovecraft's "I am Providence"; some summarise the poet's tragic life (e.g. John Keats's "Here lies One Whose Name was writ in Water" *or Branko Miljković's* "Ubi me prejaka reč" / Killed by a word too strong); whereas others may contain a warning, as is the case with Shakespeare's epitaph (although his authorship has been questioned), or take on a comical note, a recent example being Spike Milligan's gravestone quip ("Dúirt mé leat go raibh mé breoite" / I told you I was ill) which was declared as the UK's favourite epitaph (Roberts 2012).

Rarely do we find examples of ante-mortem epitaphs, i.e. the ones that the writers chose by themselves, as is the case with J.R.R. Tolkien. Another example includes the inscription Thomas Hardy drafted for his own tomb at St Michael's Church, Stinsford ("Here rests also Thomas Hardy") but it would prove short-lived given the fact that soon after his death, his remains were transferred to Poets' Corner in Westminster Abbey, contrary to the author's wish. Hardy's heart remained at the original burial site, but the original epitaph was replaced with the one Sir Sydney Cockerell found to be more "appropriate": "Here lies the heart of Thomas Hardy" (Haslam 2009, 172). As for Tolkien, he wanted the names of his fictional characters Beren and Lúthien added to his and Edith's names on their joint grave at Wolvercote Cemetery in Oxford. The examples where a quotation or a verse by an author were used as an epitaph are numerous, but so far we have found no examples similar to Tolkien's epitaph, where authors identify with their literary characters in such a manner. In this light, Tolkien's gravestone seems to be rare, if not unique, at least to our knowledge, and this identification deserves to be further highlighted.

A Striking Identification

Tolkien and his wife Edith are buried at Wolvercote Cemetery in the north-west of Oxford. Their grave is marked by a simple granite tombstone, which contains a discrete carved cross and the inscriptions "Edith Mary Tolkien / Lúthien / 1889–1971" and "John Ronald Reuel Tolkien / Beren / 1892–1973". Edith died on 29th November 1971 in Bournemouth; after that Tolkien returned to live in Oxford where he visited Edith's grave every Sunday after attending Mass in Headington (Scull & Hammond 2017, 930).

Seven months after Edith's sudden passing, in a letter to his son Christopher written on 11th July 1972, Tolkien states that he decided to sort out the inscription on their grave, expressing his wish to have Lúthien carved beneath Edith's name and years of birth and death.

I have at last got busy about Mummy's grave . ... The inscription I should like is:

EDITH MARY TOLKIEN
1889-1971

Lúthien

: brief and jejune except for *Lúthien*, which says for me more than a multitude of words: for she was (and knew she was) my Lúthien.*

July 13. Say what you feel, without reservation, about this addition. I began this under the stress of great emotion & regret – and in any case I am afflicted from time to time (increasingly) with an overwhelming sense of bereavement. I need advice. Yet I hope none of my children will feel that the use of this name is a sentimental fancy. It is at any rate not comparable to the quoting of pet names in obituaries. I never called Edith *Lúthien* – but she was the source of the story that in time became the chief pan of *The Silmarillion*. It was first conceived in a small woodland glade filled with hemlocks at Roos in Yorkshire (where I was for a brief time in command of an outpost of the Humber Garrison in 1917, and she was able to live with me for a while). In those days her hair was raven, her skin clear, her eyes brighter than you have seen them, and she could sing – and dance. (*Letters*, Letter 340, 420)

The addition of Lúthien's name was clearly very important to Tolkien as a homage to Edith who inspired one of the fundamental stories in *The Silmarillion*. The event of her dancing for him in a small woodland glade filled with hemlocks at Roos in Yorkshire was a memory he cherished for the rest of his life, a memory so strong that he immortalised it through his writings, and finally, through the inscriptions on their joint grave. In the letter he goes on to say that he would like Christopher to know more about the sufferings of their childhoods and youth which inevitably affected their adulthood, but never dimmed the memories of their youthful love. The passage ends with another affirmation of the importance of said memory:

For ever (especially when alone) we still met in the woodland glade, and went hand in hand many times to escape the shadow of imminent death before our last parting. (*Letters*, Letter 340, 421)

Picture 1. Tolkien's grave at Wolvercote Cemetery in Oxford, September 2020. Photo by courtesy of Mike Percival.

The tale of Beren and Lúthien is well known to Tolkien scholars and fans, but we will summarise it briefly – it tells of the love between a mortal man, Beren, and an immortal Elf-maiden, Lúthien, and the obstacles they faced in order to be together. The first version of the story was written in 1917, the same year Edith danced for Tolkien in Roos. As already mentioned, that event was an inspiration for the encounter of Beren and Lúthien – Beren falls in love with the daughter of king Thingol and Melian who was "the most beautiful of all the Children of Ilúvatar", when he sees her dancing in a hemlock glade (*Silmarillion*, 'Of Beren and Lúthien', 193). Lúthien's father did not want to give her hand in marriage to a mortal man and set a seemingly impossible task on Beren – to bring him a Silmaril from the Iron Crown of Morgoth. After many difficulties and sacrifices, the quest turned out to be successful beyond all odds, leading to the first marriage between a man and an Elf, but also to Beren's death. Unable to deal with the death of her beloved, Lúthien also died, lamenting before Mandos, the ruler of the spirits of the slain and one of the Valar, over her ill fate. As Mandos was moved to pity, the lovers were eventually reunited and granted another life as mortals. The story in a way reflects all the obstacles Tolkien and Edith faced to be together, but first and foremost it is a reference to their youthful and undying love. As Tom Shippey noted, it remained deeply personal for Tolkien throughout his life, leading to his final wish to commemorate it in stone, thus establishing "a striking identification" (Shippey, 2010, ch. V, sec. 4) between the author and his fictional characters.

The lasting significance of the story was also addressed and emphasised by Christopher Tolkien himself in the Preface of *Beren and Lúthien*, published exactly one hundred years after the tale was first conceived. Assuming (wrongly) that it was to be the last of his father's writings he edited and published, he revealed that the tale of Beren and Lúthien was "chosen *in memoriam*" because of its "deeply-rooted presence" in Tolkien's life (*B&L*, 16).

Bearing in mind everything already stated, it is obvious that Tolkien's grave can be interpreted on several levels. Its most basic function, intrinsic to all graves, is to keep the memory of the deceased alive by providing to those closest to them, i.e. their family and friends, a place to recollect and commemorate them through repeated visits, and it seems that Tolkien and Edith's grave is well cared for by the family. The role of the family in memorising a lost family member also comes forward in Tolkien's need to explain his choice of the epitaph to his children, a choice which extended the evocative reach of their personal names to his legendarium. The story of Beren and Lúthien was not fully known nor published at the time (besides mentions in *The Lord of the Rings*), so his desire to affirm this connection through inscriptions on their grave gained an increased significance after *The Silmarillion* was published in 1977.

Apart from the inscribed names and years, the symbol of the cross engraved above Edith's name must be mentioned, as well as the simplicity of the monument and its location in the area of the cemetery reserved for Roman Catholics – they all point to the Christian context which was of utmost importance to Tolkien. Thus the grave connects and commemorates some of the things he cherished the most in life: his faith, his wife, and his work.

Finally, due to Tolkien's popularity, his grave has grown into a distinctive pilgrimage site. We mentioned that modern cemeteries have been the centres of individual and collective remembrance since the end of the 18th and start of the 19th century and that people's desire to pay respects to their beloved authors has brought about the practice of visiting their graves, very much alive today. The following section investigates contemporary visitors' reception of Tolkien's grave and memory practices related to it, ranging from individual, private visits and acts of remembrance to organised commemorative acts, exemplified by the ceremony of Enyalië, the concluding event of Oxonmoot.

Contemporary reception of the site

In order to analyse the contemporary reception of the grave and its importance in terms of remembering Tolkien, we will present some of the results of an online survey conducted in January 2021 which targeted participants who visited Tolkien-related places in the UK. 500 responses were gathered and among them, 315 respondents visited Tolkien's grave (63%).

A part of the survey was specifically designed for the respondents who visited the grave in order to discover what that experience meant for them. They were asked five questions which revealed their impressions and attitudes towards the location, the grave itself, and the inscriptions on it.

Respondents were asked to assess how important to them visiting Tolkien's grave was in comparison to other Tolkien-related locations in the UK (Chart 1). As demonstrated in Chart 1, for the majority of respondents visiting Tolkien's grave was extremely important. On a scale of 1 to 5, 1 being the least important and 5 the most important, almost half of the respondents said it was the most important location to visit, and additional 35% said it was very important, which goes to show that 85% of the people who visited the grave experience it as an especially significant site of memory. At the same time, that represents more than half of the total number of participants who visited Tolkien-related places in the UK (266 out of 500), which is also indicative of this location's importance and fans' inclination to visit it.

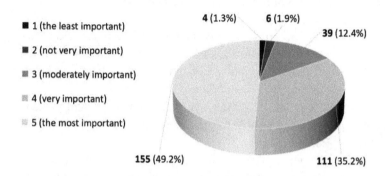

- 1 (the least important)
- 2 (not very important)
- 3 (moderately important)
- 4 (very important)
- 5 (the most important)

4 (1.3%)   6 (1.9%)

39 (12.4%)

155 (49.2%)

111 (35.2%)

Chart 1. How important to you was the visit to Tolkien's grave when compared to other Tolkien-related locations in the UK?

The respondents were further asked to pick a favourite location among the ones they visited and explain why they chose it as their favourite. 125 respondents replied that their favourite was Tolkien's grave (almost 40% of the people who visited it). Among the reasons given as to why the grave was their favourite, the participants most frequently said that it was a very emotional, meaningful, and moving experience for them to be able to pay respects to their beloved author at his grave. They usually pointed out that the place was peaceful, quiet, private, and thought provoking, and that it was the place where they felt the most connected and closest to Tolkien. A number of them said they felt humbled, and liked that the grave was simple, but well-cared for. Fifteen participants mentioned the names of Beren and Lúthien as the reason they loved the place, some of them were familiar with their existence on the gravestone prior to the visit, some were surprised by the inscriptions, but all of them found them deeply meaningful and moving. Some of the indicative answers are:

1. Tolkien's grave is my favourite. The place is so very calm and peaceful, and yet you can feel that it's often visited. It's popular but not crowded. Perfect. (K.M., Russia, 35)

2. The grave. That was a very emotional moment to stand there and be able to thank him personally. (Non-binary, 26, Germany)

3. Tolkien's grave. It was a long overdue pilgrimage to pay my respects to the professor and I took my soulmate with me to see where "the original" Beren & Lúthien rest. (Female, 34, USA/Finland)

4. Maybe the graves, because I was very struck that they said Beren and Lúthien. I found it very moving, and have told many people about it. (Andrea Keirstead, 61, USA)

5. The grave, probably because of the deep feeling conveyed by seeing "Beren & Lúthien" engraved on the tombstone. (Laura Martin-Gomez, 32, France)

6. The grave because it was so real and meaningful. To see their love etched in stone forever was beautiful. (Female, 43, USA)

7. The grave, it's well preserved and seems like a symbol of love. My partner proposed to me there, so now there is a personal connection. (M.Z., 30, UK)

8. Visiting Tolkien's grave in Oxford was really emotional, especially seeing all the messages and gifts left from all the people that he keeps touching and inspiring through

his work. (Female, 38, Italy)

9. Tolkien's grave in Wolvercote Cemetery. Because it feels like a fusion of Tolkien's personal life and his 'sub-creation'. I think it is the most important place in the world related to Tolkien. (Female, 36, Japan)

These answers illustrate how deeply personal and meaningful the experience of visiting the grave can be for Tolkien fans, as well as how much the names of Beren and Lúthien contribute to its enhanced emotional effect, for it is a site where not only Tolkien and Edith are present, but also his fictional world, evoked by a simple, but powerful reference. This double presence can simultaneously tap into readers' admiration and respect for the author himself and their love for his writings. This "fusion of Tolkien's personal life and his 'sub-creation'" for many visitors makes the grave the most important Tolkien-related place in the world (answer no. 9 above).

The participants were asked to describe their motivation for visiting the grave and the circumstances of their visit. The most common answer pertaining to motivation was "to pay respects". Many descriptions of the circumstances of the visit are also telling of the emotional impact and significance of the visit for the fans, some wanting to do it for years and perceiving it as a quest or pilgrimage, seeing the grave as the best place to express their gratitude and appreciation of Tolkien. Several visitors responded that the grave had "a sacred character" for them and that it resembled a shrine due to numerous tokens of devotion put on the grave by fans. This practice of leaving tributes at the site was praised by some because it made evident for them that other people visited the grave and shared their passion and respect for Tolkien, which underlines the social component involved in the reception of the place even during individual visits (also see answer no. 1 below). Nine respondents said that visiting the grave was a pilgrimage-like endeavour for them, and their accounts further emphasise the special status of the site as the main spot where people pay their respects and honour the memory of their favourite author:

1. It was a pilgrimage. To visit both him and Edith at once was a great honor, an experience given further weight by the thousands of like-minded pilgrims who had sang, wept, and contemplated at that exact spot for so many years. (R.C.W., 27, USA)

2. Tolkien's grave was like a mini pilgrimage for me. He has formed a large part of my life and I had the opportunity to visit when I sent to Oxford for the first time with my parents. It was a very moving experience and I feel humbled to have spent some time in his presence. (Elizabeth Cavanagh, 29, UK)

3. I actually visited three times. Once alone, once to show a friend, and once as part of a group excursion. My motivation when visiting by myself was mainly a desire to see all I could in Oxford that was Tolkien related while I was studying there. I suppose there was some element of solemnity and significance to visiting the grave itself. I hesitate to use the word pilgrimage because I was not spiritually motivated, but there was an element of that: a purposeful journey undertaken to visit a site of emotional significance. (S.W.R., 25, USA)

4. As a fan for many years, I perceived it as a Quest or pilgrimage - being there on the morning of Bilbo's birthday. (Female, 31, Denmark)

5. It was a cultural pilgrimage. I read some lines from T*he Children of Hùrin* on his grave. I believe it was some kind of metaleptical and transcendental experience. I'll definitely do it again! (H.G., 25, France) (Picture 2)

Picture 2. The participant H.G. from France during his visit to Tolkien's grave in 2019. Photo by courtesy of H.G.

A number of respondents sang or read something from Tolkien's works on the occasion or planned their visit to the grave on symbolic dates, e.g. Bilbo and Frodo's birthday:

1. I wanted to pay my respects. My brother and I went on September 22 (Hobbit day); the Tolkien Society held an event there but we ended up going as they dispersed and having a quiet moment. We both got emotional a little and sang "Roads go ever ever on" as we left. Tolkien was a huge inspiration to both of us and it was surreal to be at his grave site. (Female, 27, UK)

2. My fiancé and I were in Oxford for the 2018 Tolkien exhibition at the Bodleian. We planned to visit his grave while we were there because we both love his work. Tolkien has been part of my life since I was 7 years old and my Bachelor's thesis was about the legendarium. So it was very meaningful for me to visit his grave. While we were there we read the meeting of Beren and Lúthien from the Lays of Beleriand. (Evangeline Pousson, 28, USA)

3. I was young at that time (the Peter Jackson's movies didn't exist) and went to England especially to "walk in J.R.R. Tolkien's footsteps", during one year of philosophy studies at the University of Birmingham. (I also choose to go there 'cause of Tolkien). The first time I went to Oxford, I ended the day by going to visit the grave. I didn't know what to expect and was quite surprised to see the "Beren and Lúthien" inscriptions. I must say it was quite moving. (Gelydrihan, 43, France)

It is interesting that certain people mentioned only the desire to see the names Beren and Lúthien inscribed on the grave as their motivation. For a number of visitors it was a long-overdue dream come true, and they described their motivation and experiences in length, like these two participants from Poland and Mexico:

1. I remembered thinking that I would like to go visit his grave right after I finished reading *LOTR* for the first time (18 years ago when I was 12). When I decided to go to the exhibition I knew I would go to his grave. Took the bus from Oxford and brought white roses

with me. Stayed for about 10 minutes since there were some workers in the Cemetery. Left 9 of the roses and took one with me (my mother superstition on gifting odd numbers of flowers), which is now on my Tolkien bookshelf (transported back on the airplane in an empty water bottle). It was nice to make my 12 year old version dream come true, especially since then I haven't really believed it would ever be possible. (K.W., 30, Poland)

2. I visited to the grave just to say thank you for all that Tolkien's work has meant in my life. I waited this travel since I was 13 (when I visited the grave I was 28) after I read the Tolkien's biography written by Humphrey Carpenter in my home in Guadalajara, México. It was a sunny but cold day in Oxford, my girlfriend was with me and after some photos she left me alone in the grave for one hour. Through all this time I thought of the places and moments where I read his books, nothing else. The previous day I visited Birmingham and cut some leaves in Moseley Bog and the Sarehole Mill area and I put these leaves on the grave because I thought he would love to have some part of the land that he loved near his mortal remains. (Damián de Jesús Castillo Preciado, 29, Mexico)

These answers are similar to those comparing the visit to a pilgrimage, and they call attention to the significance of material mementos that some fans leave at the site. The second answer is especially interesting for the choice of the objects left on the grave – "some leaves from Moseley Bog and Sarehole Mill area".

Based on all the answers gained via the survey, the rituals of homage enacted at Tolkien and Edith's grave range from silent contemplation to singing, reciting, reading excerpts from Tolkien's works silently or aloud, or leaving wreaths, flowers, notes, drawings, coins, figurines, jewellery, and other tributes, as well as taking some mementos, which are usually photos, but several participants also mentioned gravestone rubbings, stones, or plants.

The respondents were asked if they put anything on the grave, and 189 (60%) of them replied that they did not; 54 (17.1%) left flowers; 25 (8%) left some notes, letters or poems; 16 (5.1%) left coins; stones or jewellery were left by 8 participants each; several respondents mentioned religious objects, certain national symbols, drawings, books, figurines and other less common tokens of affection. 20 respondents said that they did not personally leave anything on the grave, but participated in wreath laying during collective visits, whether organised by the Tolkien Society or by Tolkien-related societies and groups from other countries.

In the third question participants were asked to describe their impressions of the location and the grave itself (Chart 2), and both were most commonly labelled beautiful and peaceful, while the visiting experience itself was most frequently characterised as moving and emotional.

Terms that appear in half of all the answers describing the grave are: simple, ordinary, humble, modest, unpretentious, unassuming, understated, appropriate, respectful, private, quiet, peaceful, calm, serene. The second most common way of describing it included the words lovely, beautiful, nice, gorgeous, magical, perfect, impressive, whilst some others chose the terms touching, emotional, and moving. Significant number of participants noted that the grave was well kept and cared for, as well as often visited. 48 respondents liked the flowers, notes and other tokens of appreciation people left on the grave as an expression of their love, gratitude and respect, and, as noted previously, several answers compared it with a shrine and said it had a sacred character due to the things left on it. On the other hand, certain people disliked this practice and found it inappropriate and disrespectful. Some respondents remarked that the grave was easy to find, but others found it difficult, however, a significant number of people pointed out that the signposts leading to the grave were very helpful.

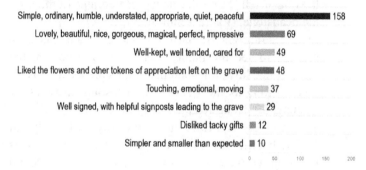

Chart 2. Describe your impressions of the location and the grave itself.

Only ten participants found it simpler and smaller than expected, whilst most of the others liked its simplicity and found it appropriate and in accordance with Tolkien's own beliefs and values:

1. It's unassuming and unprepossessing. I rather liked that about it. The simplicity felt appropriate. It was a little difficult to find but there was some signage. Each time I went there were a few flowers or something left by

others. It's a quiet spot for peaceful thought. It brings home that Tolkien was a real, complicated person. (S.W.R., 25, USA)

2. I was moved by how humble and unassuming it was, and moved to tears by the Beren / Lúthien inscriptions. (Chris Newton, 34, UK)

3. Seemed tucked away, but not too hard to find. Love that it has plants as growing things are appropriate for Tolkien. Always interested to see what other mementos fans have left. Love the names Beren and Lúthien on the headstone. (Laura Schmidt, 39, USA)

4. I was reading The Silmarillion that time so it was extra moving to see the names Beren and Lúthien on the grave. I like how quiet and near fields the location is - it seems fitting as the writer's final resting place. (Jody Cheung, 30, Hong Kong)

5. The cemetery is a little out of the way on the edge of Oxford but beautiful and well maintained. The signposts to the grave were useful or I might have never found it. The grave seemed very often visited - there were flowers left on it, and a couple of tribute notes from fans. I'd have left one myself but it was raining. (Tas Cooper, 30, UK)

6. Very ordinary except for the names Beren and Lúthien. But that was the magic of it. Knowing that he created such magic in literature and seeing something as humble as a tombstone and knowing it meant so much more. (David Tracy, 46, Canada)

As seen from these examples, many visitors said that they loved the names of Beren and Lúthien on the gravestone, and were even moved to tears by them. As David Tracy from Canada put it, although the monument itself may look "very ordinary", the whole "magic of it" rests upon seeing such a humble tombstone but knowing it means "so much more".

The next question posed in the survey investigated participants' opinions about the names of Beren and Lúthien being on the gravestone in greater detail (Chart 3).

The most frequent terms used in this context were touching, moving, emotional, and poignant, followed by various ways of saying that the inscriptions are symbolic of Tolkien and Edith's relationship, an expression of their love, a message of love and respect, a nice homage or parallel to their love story which inspired the story of Beren and Lúthien who also had to overcome many obstacles in order to finally be together. In a similar vein, many respondents said that the inscriptions show how profoundly Tolkien related to his writings, and emphasise the connection between his life and work, being a lovely testimony of his love for both Edith and his sub-creation.

Many described it as beautiful, lovely, romantic, and sweet and said that they loved it. A significant number of participants said that it was appropriate and fitting, and 10% of the respondents stressed that it was appropriate and meaningful since the appearance of the monument and the inscriptions were his own choice. Some found it to be a nice personal touch, as well as poetic, inspiring, perfect, and fantastic, whilst some pointed out that it makes the story of Beren and Lúthien even more beautiful, powerful, significant, and real. Only a few people found it surprising or had no opinions or feelings about it.

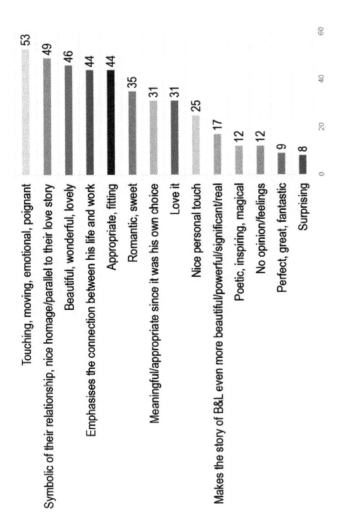

Chart 3. What do you think about the names of Beren and Lúthien being on the gravestone?

Some of the most indicative answers are cited to illustrate all previously said. They show that for many visitors the epitaph provides an insight into how deeply personal the story of Beren and Lúthien was for Tolkien, and sheds a new light on its importance within the legendarium:

1. By reading The Silmarillion I didn't get the impression the story was so central to Tolkien's tales of the First age, this information put it in a different perspective for me. (B.B., 43, Slovenia)

2. I like that names are there. I like the connection between JRRT's work and world he created - and his personal life, how he found ideas for his books in everyday life and his own experience. So names somehow seem to complete the circle. (K.M., 35, Russia)

3. It was touching on two levels: too see how much Tolkien loved his wife (that such a beautiful and inspiring character was inspired by her) and secondly to see how powerfully the world of faerie was a part of Tolkien's reality. Seeing these characters names on gravestones makes one almost believe they could truly have existed. (Chris Newton, 34, UK)

4. I think it is a testament to their love for one another, something beautiful and personal that we can understand by reading the story now that it has been fully published. (Katey Smith, 31, USA)

5. I think it's beautiful as it represents something they both lived throughout their lives: the need to overcome odds to be together, and Tolkien's universe being part of family/work life. (Marianne Albuquerque, 46, Brazil/ UK)

6. Lovely. Shows how important and personal Tolkien's writing was to him. (J.G., 28, Canada)

7. I think it speaks of the deep love they had for each other. It moved me. It also showed me how much his work meant to them in their own lives. (Female, 66, UK)

8. I found it very touching; perhaps the most touching about the grave. I even decided to sit by and read the chapter "Beren and Lúthien" from The Silmarillion. It was so beautiful and pure to see the love between Tolkien and his wife was immortalised so creatively through his works. (Silmarien, 27, UK)

9. It's beautiful. The Professor saw him and his beloved wife as Beren and Lúthien, the most beautiful love story in Tolkien lore. Both J.R.R. Tolkien and Edith had to overcome obstacles throughout their lives just like Beren and Lúthien. (E.N.G., 32, Spain)

10. It's quite fitting. That legend is one of the cornerstones of his mythology and it's very wholesome to see the names knowing that Tolkien was inspired by Edith's dancing for the moment when Beren finds Lúthien." (Ricardo Figueroa, 29, Mexico)

11. I always thought it was very ballsy and brave of Tolkien to choose that. (F.J.P., 53, USA)

12. I think it's the ultimate fantasy homage. The connection of his works and his real life manifested in stone. (Female, 28, Germany)

As some of the respondents pointed out, going back to Shippey's remark, the addition of fictional characters' names to his and Edith's name was "a striking identification" indeed, "the ultimate fantasy homage" and a brave decision, but seen by most fans as appropriate, profound, and beautiful. Also, it should be emphasised once more that such an identification is rare, if not unique, in the context of the broader culture of writers' epitaphs.

An illustrative example which can be used to recapitulate the preceding and summarise the whole visiting experience of many fans who took the survey are the answers of Hannah Middlebrook (24, USA). She said that the grave was her favourite location, because:

> …it really brought home the personhood of Tolkien for me. In my head, he's this huge literary figure who created such a detailed legendarium and changed the fantasy genre, but he was a person too, buried here. … I liked how quiet it was. No bright showy thing saying "Here it is!" It felt like visiting the grave of a family member rather than a famous person. And people had left various trinkets that showed just how many other people had come that day to pay their respects. A good feeling of connection.

Describing her motivation, Hannah explained that she knew Tolkien's headstone had Beren and Lúthien on it and that she always wanted to see that, and pay her respects, further commenting about the inscription: "Makes my heart happy. I've read *The Silmarillion* and it makes the story and my knowledge of Tolkien's life more special knowing that those stories were intertwined with his own life and feelings."

Therefore, starting from experiencing the site as more intimate and "real" than other Tolkien-related places, a location where an individual may get the closest to Tolkien and thank him for creating an imaginary world which plays such an impressive role in the lives of so many people, simultaneously feeling connected to all those people by seeing their flowers, notes and other mementos, and finally, seeing it as an almost sacred place where his and his wife's mortal remains lie under a tombstone which connects and commemorates his personal life and his sub-creation – it is not surprising that all these meanings intertwined leave a strong emotional impact on many visitors.

When considering the emotional impact of Tolkien's grave, there is a collective annual event which determines the reception of the site for a significant number of visitors and represents an important part of commemorating Tolkien at this location. It is the ceremony of Enyalië,[3] organised by the Tolkien Society as the concluding part of Oxonmoot, the Society's event held every September on a weekend close to Bilbo and Frodo's birthday. On the last day of Oxonmoot, on Sunday morning, the attendees take a coach trip to Wolvercote Cemetery, where the ceremony consists of the Chair of the Society reading something from Tolkien's works, wreath laying, and singing of *Namarië*.[4]

82 out of 315 participants said that they visited Tolkien-related locations in the UK as a part of the Tolkien Society events, and among them 61 (19.4%) mentioned Oxonmoot (47) and Enyalië (29). Many who attended the event can testify that it is a very emotional occasion which frequently involves crying elicited by the Chair's reading or singing of Namarië, as some of the respondents remarked. If describing the ceremony itself and their impressions of the event, they mostly used the terms moving, touching, overwhelming, and beautiful:

---

3. The word Enyalië means "remembrance" or "memory" in Quenya.
4. https://www.tolkiensociety.org/society/events/oxonmoot/enyalie/

1. Visited as part of Oxonmoot many times over 30 years. The first time I was anxious that the ceremony would be uncomfortable, but went because visiting the grave felt important, the most direct link with The Professor. It turned out to be deeply moving, an essential part of the weekend. (Silivrien, 61, UK)

2. As part of the activities at Oxonmoot in 2018, I attended the ceremony commemorating Tolkien's life with many Tolkien Society members. It was a very beautiful and reverent occasion. (John David Cofield, 64, USA)

For some people Enyalië is the only way they have experienced the site, and, if compared to private visits to the grave, it provides a significantly different experience, collective, ceremonial and ritualistic in nature. As Harm Schelhaas (57, Netherlands) observed: "I'm always there at Enyalië, so impressions are more those of the ceremonial occasion." Ritual practices are a powerful means of establishing culturally constituted and socially shared memories, and collective participation in visiting the grave during Oxonmoot further elevates the feeling of connection and sharing with other fans, implicit in the case of individual visitors who get the sense of connection from the objects they encounter at the location.

Finally, a rare attitude exemplified by the following quotation deserves to be taken into account, as it was expressed by three respondents who pointed out that they were only interested in the books, not so much in the author himself, so they had no emotional response to the grave:

I was at Oxonmoot and other people were going. I wasn't particularly interested in going, and was close to not doing so as I found the idea of visiting the grave of someone who I did not know personally a little strange. I went along more to socialise with other attendees than for any other reason. I am not really very interested in Tolkien the man - and if I am interested at all it is in his life as a professor and a writer, not in where his remains lie. I love his stories though. (JRP, 46, UK)

Nonetheless, the site has proven to impress and invoke powerful memories and emotions among the majority of admirers who visit the grave. We have seen that many respondents loved that the connection between Tolkien's private life and his works was embodied in stone and found it particularly meaningful.

Numerous individual, private ways of honouring the Professor at his grave, and the ceremony of Enyalië add new layers of meaning to the overall reception of the site. Of course, there are many modes of remembering Tolkien and his works, and the grave is only one place where this memory is kept alive, but perhaps the one where people frequently feel the closest to him (the second one being The Eagle and Child pub in Oxford according to our survey). This sense of connection is definitely enhanced by Tolkien's own decision to commemorate not only his wife and himself at their final resting place, but also his sub-creation by adding the names Beren and Lúthien as an epitaph. To many people that addition may seem ridiculous or insignificant, but not to those who know that their names mean "so much more".

Bibliography

Ariès, Philippe, *Western Attitudes Toward Death from the Middle Ages to the Present*, trans. by Patricia M. Ranum (London: Marion Boyars, 1976).

Foucault, Michel, 'Of Other Spaces (1967)', in *Heterotopia and the City: Public Space in a Postcivil Society*, ed. by Michiel Dehaene and Lieven de Cauter (London and New York: Routledge), pp. 13–29.

Haslam, Sara, 'Wessex, Literary Pilgrims and Thomas Hardy', in *Literary Tourism and Nineteenth-Century Culture*, ed. by Nicola J. Watson (Basingstoke: Palgrave Macmillan, 2009), pp. 164–174.

Nora, Pierre, 'Preface to the English Edition: From Lieux de mémoire to Realms of Memory', in *Realms of Memory: Rethinking the French Past: Conflicts and Divisions*, vol. I, ed. by Pierre Nora (New York: Columbia University Press, 1996), pp. XV–XVII.

Pliberšek, Lidija et al., 'From Burial Spaces to Pilgrimage Sites: The Changing Role of European Cemeteries', in *Dark Tourism and Pilgrimage*, ed. by Daniel H. Olsen and Maximiliano E. Kostanje (Boston, Massachusetts: CABI, 2019), 75–84.

Roberts, Hannah, '"I told you I was ill..." Spike Milligan's gravestone quip is nation's favourite epitaph', *Daily Mail*, 18 May 2012, https://www.dailymail.co.uk/news/article-2146080/ Spike-Milligan-epitaph-Gravestone-quip-nations-favourite.

html [Accessed 30 January 2021]

Scull, Christina, and Hammond, Wayne G., *The J.R.R. Tolkien Companion and Guide. Reader's Guide. Part II*, (London: HarperCollins, 2017)

Seaton, A.V., 'Thanatourism's Final Frontiers? Visits to Cemeteries, Churchyards and Funerary Sites as Sacred and Secular Pilgrimage', *Tourism Recreation Research* 27/2 (2002), pp. 73–82.
—— 'Death', in *Key Words for Travel Writing Studies: A Critical Glossary*, ed. by Charles Forsdick et al. (London: Anthem Press, 2019), pp. 66–68.

Shippey, Tom, *J.R.R. Tolkien: Author of the Century*, (London: HarperCollins, 2010), epub edition.

Tolkien, J.R.R., *The Silmarillion*, ed. by Christopher Tolkien (London: HarperCollins, 1999).
—— *The Letters of J.R.R. Tolkien*, ed. by Humphrey Carpenter (Boston – New York: Houghton Mifflin Harcourt, 2000, 19811).
—— *Beren and Lúthien*, ed. by Christopher Tolkien (London: HarperCollins, 2017).

Toussaint, Stéphanie, and Decrop, Daniel, 'Père-Lachaise cemetery: Between Dark Tourism and Heterotopic Consumption', in *Dark Tourism and Place Identity: Managing and Interpreting Dark Places*, ed. by Leanne White and Elspeth Frew (London – New York, 2013), pp. 13–27.

About the Contributors

Jelena Filipovic works as a lecturer in the Department of Modern English Literature at the Heinrich-Heine-University Düsseldorf, Germany. She obtained her B.A. in English Studies and Political Sciences and her M.A. in Comparative Studies in English and American Language, Literature and Culture. She is currently working on her PhD project titled "Satanic Politics: Literary Sovereignty in Milton, Blake, and Tolkien". In October 2019 she presented her paper "Tolkien's Dark Lord as a Political Figure" at the 16th German Tolkien Seminar held at the Friedrich-Schiller University, for which she also received a stipend from the German Tolkien Society.

Marie Bretagnolle is a French doctoral student whose work focuses on the illustrations created for British and American editions of Tolkien's Middle-earth texts. She is preparing her PhD under the joint supervision of Vincent Ferré, a renowned Tolkien specialist (Paris Est-Créteil university), and Isabelle Gadoin, who specialises in text-image relationships (Poitiers university). She has presented her work at various Tolkien Society events since 2019, interviewed Alan Lee for the French national Library in February 2020, and is the host of Nerdanel's workshop, a Tolkien Society smial for artists.

Nick Groom is best known for his books on national identity, environmentalism, and the Gothic – including *The Union Jack* (2006, revised edn 2017), *The Seasons* (2013), *The*

Gothic (2012), and *The Vampire* (2018, revised edn 2020), as well as editions of novels such as Matthew Lewis's *The Monk* (2016) and Mary Shelley's *Frankenstein* (2018). He has also published several essays on Tolkien's work, covering areas such as Tolkien's debt to the English literary tradition (2014, revised edn 2021) and links between *The Lord of the Rings* and William Golding's *Lord of the Flies* (2017). He is Professor of Literature in English at the University of Macau, and has previously taught at the universities of Oxford, Bristol, Stanford, Chicago, and Exeter.

Mina Lukić (1988) is a teaching assistant at the Faculty of Philosophy of the University of Priština in Kosovska Mitrovica. She obtained BA and MA degree in Art History at the University of Belgrade, where she is a PhD student, specialising in museology, heritage and cultural memory studies, researching the modes of remembering Tolkien.

Dejan Vukelić (1986) is a research assistant at the Mathematical Institute of the Serbian Academy of Sciences and Arts. He obtained BA in English Language and Literature (University of Kragujevac) and MA in Art History (University of Belgrade). Currently a PhD student in art history, specialising in heritage and cultural memory studies, with particular interest in mechanisms of cultural forgetting, Serbian dynastic heritage and issues of destroyed, endangered, expatriated and forgotten cultural monuments.